Institute of Classical Architecture & Classical America
The Classical America Series in Art and Architecture

DOVER PUBLICATIONS, INC.

Greek and Roman Architecture in Classic Drawings by Hector d'Espouy
Monumental Classic Architecture in Great Britain and Ireland by Albert E. Richardson
The Secrets of Good Design for Artists, Artisans and Craftors by Burl N. Osburn

GUILD FOUNDATION PRESS

The Original Green: Unlocking the Mystery of True Sustainability by Stephen A. Mouzon

W. W. NORTON & CO.

The Golden City by Henry Hope Reed
The American Vignola by William R. Ware (also available as a Dover reprint)
The Library of Congress: Its Architecture and Decoration by Herbert Small
The New York Public Library: Its Architecture and Decoration by Henry Hope Reed
The Elements of Classical Architecture by George Gromort
The Architecture of the Classical Interior by Steven W. Semes
Classical Architecture for the Twenty-First Century: An Introduction to Design by J. François Gabriel
The United States Capitol: Its Architecture and Decoration by Henry Hope Reed
Arthur Brown Jr.: Progressive Classicist by Jeffrey T. Tillman
The Future of the Past: A Conservation Ethic for Architecture, Urbanism, and Historic Preservation by
   Steven W. Semes
Comparative Architectural Details: A Selection from Pencil Points 1932–1937, edited by Milton
   Wilfred Grenfell
The Theory of Mouldings by C. Howard Walker and Richard Sammons
Building Details by Frank M. Snyder, Introduction by Peter Pennoyer and Anne Walker
The Study of Architectural Design by John F. Harbeson, John Blatteau, and Sandra L. Tatman
Edwin Howland Blashfield: Master American Muralist, edited by Mina Rieur Weiner

PRINCETON ARCHITECTURAL PRESS

Antiquities of Athens by James Stuart and Nicholas Revett, Introduction by Frank Salmon
Basilique de Saint Pierre et Le Vaticane by Paul M. Letarouilly, Introduction by Ingrid Rowland

RIZZOLI

Bricks and Brownstone: The New York Row House 1783–1929 by Charles Lockwood

SAN MATEO COUNTY HISTORICAL ASSOCIATION

Carolands: Ernest Sanson, Achille Duchêne, Willis Polk by Michael Middleton Dwyer; produced by
   Charles Davey

STERLING PUBLISHING

Get Your House Right, Architectural Elements to Use & Avoid by Marianne Cusato & Ben Pentreath
   with Richard Sammons and Léon Krier

For a complete list of titles in the Classical America Series, visit www.classicist.org

INSTITUTE OF
CLASSICAL ARCHITECTURE
& CLASSICAL AMERICA

The Institute of Classical Architecture & Classical America (ICA&CA)
is dedicated to the classical tradition in architecture and the allied arts in the United States.
Inquiries about the ICA&CA mission and programs are welcome and should be addressed
to:

The Institute of Classical Architecture & Classical America
www.classicist.org

FENCES, GATES &
GARDEN HOUSES

Gate to Chapin House
Rochester

Lyon - Chapin House, Fence,
Rochester, N. Y.

Fences, Gates & Garden Houses

A Book of Designs with Measured Drawings

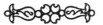

Carl F. Schmidt

Dover Publications, Inc.
Mineola, New York

in Association with The Institute of Classical Architecture & Classical America

Bibliographical Note

This Dover edition, first published in 2012, is an unabridged republication of
the work originally self-published by the author in Rochester, New York, in 1963.

Library of Congress Cataloging-in-Publication Data

Schmidt, Carl Frederick, 1894–
    Fences, gates, and garden houses : a book of designs with measured draw-
ings / Carl F. Schmidt. — Dover ed.
       p. cm.
    Originally published: Rochester, N.Y. : Carl F. Schmidt, 1963.
    Includes index.
    ISBN-13: 978-0-486-48915-5
    ISBN-10: 0-486-48915-9
    1. Fences—United States—Designs and plans. 2. Gates—United States—
Designs and plans. 3. Garden structures—United States—Designs and plans.
I. Title.

NA8390.S3 2012
717—dc23

                               2011045651

Manufactured in the United States by Courier Corporation
48915901
www.doverpublications.com

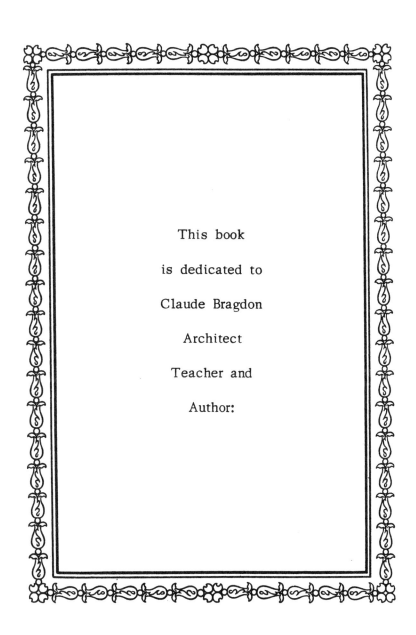

This book

is dedicated to

Claude Bragdon

Architect

Teacher and

Author:

INTRODUCTION

From 1915 when he was a student at Cornell University to the present day Carl F. Schmidt, architect and artist, has devoted nearly all his leisure to locating and recording both regional and outstanding examples of early architecture in the United States, with particular emphasis on Western New York.

Over the years Mr. Schmidt has built up an impressive collection of measured drawings, pencil sketches and photographs that now forms an invaluable record. A part of this has been drawn on to illustrate Mr. Schmidt's writings (eg. Cobblestone Architecture, 1944: Greek Revival Architecture in the Rochester area, 1946 and a series of folios of pencil sketches to scale of early doorways in and around Rochester, N. Y.). In the present volume Mr. Schmidt has again drawn on this treasure-trove to present a notable selection of measured drawings of ornamental wood fences and small garden houses, many of which are now published for the first time and will further aid the study of early architecture.

Comparatively little literature or documentary evidence is available on the subject of the wood fences that invariably enclosed the front gardens of Post-Colonial, Greek Revival and to a diminishing extent, Victorian style houses in the later eighteenth and early nineteenth centuries. A study of early paintings, prints and drawings and the few surviving original examples reveals great care was given to the design and construction of fences in relation to the house design and its ornamentation. Practical considerations dictating the enclosure of front gardens in villages and towns were sometimes eclipsed by the sheer loveliness of the fencing as it framed the area and drew the eye to the house.

The relatively short life of a wood fence exposed to the elements, estimated variously by contemparary writers at from twenty-five to forty years, unless given exceptional care, plus changing styles and other factors have combined to eliminate most original examples. We are fortunate that Carl F. Schmidt from his earliest days realized the architectural significance and charm of wood fences and garden houses and has recorded them for our enlightenment and pleasure.

Elizabeth G. Holahan

FOREWORD

Slowly but surely during my lifetime, most of the beautiful old fences and gates have disappeared. Decay and prohibitive costs of authentic replacement have deprived the youth of today and all future generations of enjoying the beautiful fences, gates and garden houses that once embellished our streets, gardens and highways.

It was during the early 1920's when I first went to New England on sketching and measuring jaunts, that I become interested in fences and gates. About ten years ago I became aware that the fences were gradually being demolished. While gathering material for some of my other books, I also measured and photographed all the fences and garden houses I could find with the idea that some day I would make them available in book form.

Many of the fences photographed and measured in this book have been destroyed. It is difficult to realize that only two old fences remain in the city of Rochester and not more than six in all Monroe County.

It is the author's hope this book may help stimulate an interest in our rapidly diminishing architectural dependencies of the past, and that a few fences, gates and garden houses will be preserved for posterity.

I want to express my gratitude to my wife, Anne Schmidt, for suggestions, correcting and typing, to Lucy Schmidt for correcting the manuscript.

Carl F. Schmidt

INDEX

INDEX

FENCES, GATES and GARDEN HOUSES

Never shall I forget walking through Essex, Federal and Chestnut Streets in Salem, Massachusettes in the 1920's, when most of the beautiful fences were still in place. In no other city were the streets lined with so many beautiful examples of wood fencing. Here privacy and a proper regard for one's neighbors were expressed in faultless fashion. Newburyport, Portsmouth and Litchfield were not far behind; many other New England villages could boast of beautiful wooden fences.

The word "fence" is derived from the Latin "defendo," meaning to defend. It could mean any kind of construction for the purpose of enclosing an area for defence; as a bank of earth, a wall, a ditch, a paling, railing or hedge. In America crude fences or stone walls were first used as a protection against wandering cattle and hogs. Each householder had to provide and maintain his own fences.

At first fencing probably consisted of split rails or rough boards. We are all familiar with the zigzag rail fence, sometines also called "worm fence." Hundreds of miles of "dry-stone-wall" fences were built by expert craftsmen whose trade was the source of their name-dry-stone-wall masons.

In this book we are interested only in the beautiful wood fences, the best of which were erected in the years between the Revolutionary War and 1825, when the master craftsmen did not deem it beneath their dignity to devote sufficient time for the study of fences. They had the determination and the desire to excell, to do their best even in the smallest details. We do not have the time in our hurried life to take pains with the minor details, and that is the principal reason why so much of our modern architecture is crude and ill considered.

The fences varied from the very simple to the most elaborate designs as indicated in the photographs and measured drawings, depending on the financial ability and the individual taste of the owners and builders. However, elaborate or simple the designs and the various parts were always well proportioned and the mouldings appropriate to the material, wood. The fence was usually an integral part of the entire design, an introduction to the details and motifs to be found in the entrance and in the house itself. A fence should enhance the architecture of the house; it should express the characteristics of either lightness or strength. This our early 19th century builders ably accomplished. The delicate details of the Post-Colonial type fence are harmonious with the details of that style, whereas the Greek Revival builders achieved a strength and stability in their designs for wood fences that arouses our admiration. They developed new types of mouldings and a breadth of surface material that were consistent with the Classic spirit. During the 20th Century the fine proportions and the feeling for wood details were lost.

High solid brick walls, high fences of a combination of brick piers and wrought iron, and those made entirely of wrought iron were found frequently in Europe; these did not have a friendly or neighborly feeling and consequently never became popular in New England.

According to some early writers on house building, the fence was considered an important architectural feature. One writer states that "no residence can be properly protected, or regarded as complete without fencing."

For some reason Asher Benjamin and A. J. Downing, both of whom had a tremendous influence on American Architecture, did not look with favor on fences. This may have had a great deal to do with the gradual disappearance of this beautiful architectural dependency.

In "The Architect or Practical House Carpenter," published by Asher Benjamin in 1844, one plate is devoted to fence designs. (See plate 63 in this book). Benjamin states: "On this plate are three designs for fences, suitable for the enclosure of a country residence, which may be made of wood, when iron is not to be obtained, or when expense is to be avoided: also two designs for gates, to be made of the same material. Mouldings do not form any part of the composition of these designs. Their construction is bold and simple, and will, if well executed, produce a more chaste and pleasing effect than if the cornice, top rail and base were composed of small, trifling mouldings; and is the means of saving considerable expense."

"It is not supposed that the size of these examples will suit all situations which require the size of front fences to be varied: as, for instance, when the house is very large, and located on an elevated piece of ground, and at a considerable distance from the road: in this case, the fence should be of the largest dimensions. But if the house be small and so situated as to have a fence near it, the fence ought then to be small and low, so that it may not appear as a principal in the structure."

In his book, "A treatise on The Theory and Practice of Landscape Gardening," A. J. Downing has much to say on the subject of fences. "Fences are often among the most unsightly and offensive objects in our country seats. Some persons appear to have a passion for subdividing their grounds into a great number of fields: a process which is scarcely ever advisable even in common farms, but for which there can be no apology in elegant residences. The close proximity of fences to the house gives the whole place a confined and mean character." "The mind," says Repton, "feels a certain disgust under a sense of confinement in any situation however beautiful." "A wide-spread lawn, on the contrary, where no boundaries are conspicuous, conveys an impression of ample extent and space for enjoyment. It is frequently the case that, on that side of the house nearest the outbuildings, fences are for convenience, brought in its close neighborhood, and here they are easily concealed by plantations; but on the other sides, open and unobstructed views should be preserved, by removing all barriers not absolutely necessary.

"Nothing is more common, in the places of cockneys who become inhabitants of the country, than a display immediately around the dwelling of a spruce paling of carpentry, neatly made, and painted white or green; an abomination among the fresh fields, of which no person of taste could be guilty. To fence off a small plot around a fine house, in the midst of a lawn of fifty acres, is a perversity which we could never reconcile with even the lowest perception of beauty. An old stone wall covered with creepers and climbing plants, may become a picturesque barrier a thousand times superior to such a fence. But there is never one instance in a thousand where any barrier is necessary. Where it is desirable to separate the house from the level grass of the lawn, let it be done by an architectural terrace of stone, or a raised platform of gravel supported by turf, which will confer importance and dignity upon the building, instead of giving it a petty and trifling expression."

"Verdant hedges are elegant substitutes for stone or wooden fences, and we are surprised that their use has not been hitherto more general."

One is often amazed at the beauty of the simple fences built during the nineteenth century, especially those built during the first third of the century. Using but one or two simple mouldings, and sometimes without the use of any mouldings, the craftsmen achieved a simple rhythm and harmony of solids and voids that defies the modern designer. Plates 21, 39, 42, 43, 46 and 52 show examples of their skill.

A fence consists of a shell of boards enclosing the wood posts, a top and bottom rail with facing strips, and turned, square or flat cut-out pickets. With these elements we can achieve beauty and charm. It is the relationship of the size and height of the pickets to the space between the pickets, the relationship of picket and spacing to the width and the height of the posts, and the relationship of the post caps and their embellishments to the height and thickness of the posts that produce the beautiful proportions of a fence. Somehow our nineteenth century craftsmen sensed these refinements.

The fence at 471 Mount Hope Avenue, Rochester, New York, is an interesting Victorian example. The eight-inch square posts have chamfered edges and the tops are finished with a miniature gable or gablet. A one-half-inch thick board with a moulded edge is applied to the face of the posts.

The wood fence setting on a low stone wall that once extended along the front and Troup Street side of the Lyon-Chapin House in Rochester was in perfect harmony with the beautiful Greek Revival house. The posts were about twenty-two inches square with paneled faces, moulded caps and beautifully carved finials, as shown on plate 5. The round pickets with rounded tops were 1-1/8 inches in diameter and spaced five inches on centers.

The low wood fence resting on a seventeen-inch high stone wall in front of the Genesee Valley Club (the Erickson-Perkins House) on East Avenue in Rochester is another good example in the Greek Revival style. The entrance gate is recessed in the form of a half circle, which is a simple and effective way to create an inviting feeling. The pickets are two inches square and set four inches apart. Short posts consisting of thirteen-and-one-half-inch wide pilasters, each projecting four and one-half inches, form a post with a total width of twenty-two and one-half inches. The exposed pilasters have deeply recessed panels. See plate 6.

The only Post-Colonial type fence remaining in Monroe County is located in front of the Jewett-Pattison House in Clarkson, New York. See plate 11. The posts are only six inches square with simple moulded caps, and the pickets, one and three-sixteenths inches square with beveled tops, are set on a high solid-paneled base, about eight and one-half inches on centers. From moulded wood collars in the center of the pickets, thin wood strips extend diagonally to the center of the spaces between the pickets.

Plates 12 and 13 illustrate the fence that once enclosed Belcoda Cemetery in Monroe County. The horizontal boards diminish in width from bottom to top; the spaces between the boards increase from two and one-half inches at the bottom to five inches at the top. On each side of the gates and at each corner of the lot, posts seven and one-quarter inches square were set with moulded cast iron caps. The wide carriage gate had a wood arch supported between high posts.

Plates 20 and 22 illustrate interesting fences in Caledonia and Canawaugus, New York, in the Victorian style. They are very simple fences made without the use of mouldings and are probably the work of the same carpenter.

The fence in front of the Sackett-Ault House near Canandaigua, New York, as shown on plate 28, is in the Greek Revival spirit. The upper part of the post cap is made of moulded cast iron.

Plate 32 illustrates one of the well-known "peacock" gates in the fence in front of the Charles Waldrun House in Rensselaerville, New York. The pickets are about one and three-sixteenths inches square with beveled tops and spaced four inches on centers. The edges of the six-inch square posts are chamfered to form an octagon and the tops shaped into a ball. (See photograph, page 23) for carriage gate in the same fence.

The fence on the property of Mrs. Margaret Thompson in Claverack, New York, is a transitional design with both Greek Revival and Victorian characteristics. The one-and-one-half inch square pickets are grooved in the center of the front and rear sides so they do not appear so heavy. In the gate, the turned one-and-one-half inch pickets are alternately long and short. See plates 34 and 35.

A good example of a fence with a protective lower section is that at the Chase House, Annapolis, Maryland. A solid wood paneled section, sixteen inches high, forms the base for the pickets. The four-inch square posts are about eight feet on centers with turned acorn-shaped caps; the pickets are round, one and one-eight inches in diameter with sharp pointed tops. See plate 38.

The brick wall separating the garden from the street at the Read House in New Castle, Delaware, is four feet nine inches high with brick piers about eight feet high. The space above the wall and between the piers is filled with a two-foot-six-inch high fencing, consisting of one-and-one-quarter inch diameter balusters with rounded tops, which are spaced about five inches on centers as shown on plate 40.

The Quay House fence in Litchfield, Connecticut, is a beautiful example of the Post-Colonial type. See plate 44. It consists of turned one and one-eighth inch diameter pickets, spaced about four inches on centers. The posts are accentuated with fluted pilasters, well-proportioned caps and beautiful carved finials. The horizontal members have two small half round mouldings on the face which enhance the delicate appearance of these structural members. Raising the upper rail and increasing the height of the pickets at the posts are one of the most successful methods of tying together fence and posts into a unit.

One of the most successful fences in Salem, Massachusetts, is the one in front of the Ropes Memorial, illustrated in plate 53. The posts are faced with small fluted Ionic pilasters and finished with well-proportioned caps and urns. The upward sweep of the top rail at the posts is an ideal way to unify the low fencing with the posts. Turned pickets, one and one-eighth inches in diameter, with pine-cone endings are spaced four and three-quarters inches from center to center of pickets.

The posts of the Pierce-Nichols fence in Salem, Massachusetts, as shown on plate 55, are plain and solid looking, but the mouldings of the post caps and horizontal rails are delicate and refined. The beautifully proportioned carved urns with conventional flame top, which crown the posts, are out-standing features. The pickets are only seven-eighths of an inch square with beveled tops and are spaced five inches from center to center.

Another beautiful example in Salem, Massachusetts, is the Baldwin-Lyman fence as shown on plate 56. High ten-inch square posts, faced with narrow Ionic pilasters, increase the feeling of height in the posts. The small carved Ionic capitals, the elaborate cap mouldings of the posts, and the urns with flame tops are beautifully proportioned. The pickets are one inch square with beveled tops.

In the Ropes Memorial, the Pierce-Nichols and Baldwin-Lyman fences, we have fence design in its most beautiful and appropriate expression.

On plates 57 and 58 are shown two fences on Middle Road in Portsmouth, New Hampshire, which are usually referred to as the Cape Cod type. These fences are usually lower than we find in the rest of New England. The posts are six inches in diameter, turned and ending in ball-shaped tops. At number 546 Middle Road the pickets are one and one-quarter inches in diameter with cone-shaped tops, while those at 569 Middle Road are sawed from two and three-quarter inch wide strips of wood.

The picket fence has a light insistence on privacy; relatively speaking a solid paneled wood fence does not appear as heavy as a brick or stone wall. The Larkin-Rice House fence, in Portsmouth, New Hampshire, plate 59, is a good example of this type. This fence makes us think of a piece of cabinet work instead of a solid wall.

The fence near Hampton, New Hampshire, as shown on plate 61, is an example of simplicity, without mouldings or ornament. The eight-inch-square posts have a simple beveled cap board with a seven-eighth inch thick strip of wood under it. The top rail is made of a beveled cap over a one and three-quarter inch by three and three-quarter inch piece of wood with a small one-half inch by seven-eighths inch strip at the intersection. The fence height is divided in the center by a horizontal rail, one and three-quarters by one-and three-quarters inch, and vertically by one and one-quarter inch square pieces to form panels, which are filled with diagonal strips.

There was also a type of fencing or lattice used to separate the garden from the service yard. Plates 1 and 8 illustrate two such fences in Rochester, New York. The lower part of the fence was either solid vertical boards or closely-spaced lattice strips, and the upper part a more open lattice pattern. A cresting cut from a board, three to six inches high, was usually installed above the top rail.

We cannot end our discussion of fences without mentioning those on Cape Cod. They were low fences with turned posts about five and one-half to seven and one-half inches in diameter with the fencing between the posts consisting of three or more horizontal boards: or square, round or octagonal rails. Sometimes they were made with top and bottom rails and turned pickets. The posts varied from two and one-half to less than four feet in height, and the fences, of course, were always lower than the posts.

These fences had a distinctive character as shown on plate 62. Although referred to as the Cape Cod fence, we do find examples in other localities. (See plates 57 and 58).

GARDEN HOUSE

The garden house, sometimes called summer-house, tea house, gazebo or belvedere, was essentially of a light and delicate construction, hence its short life and scarceness today. There were two distinct types; the latticed type, in which the thin structural frames and roof were enclosed with thin interlaced lattice strips; the other, the sides of which were enclosed with wood panels and window-sash, had a solid roof. A combination of the two styles consisted of solid vertical wood boards enclosing the sides about one-third or less of their height, and the rest an interlaced lattice work. The roofs were either solid or open lattice work. The plans were square, rectangular or octagonal in form.

The garden house was used as a sheltered retreat, where one could read and meditate. They were usually located at the intersection of the paths in the center of the garden or on a knoll at one end. It provided a delightful view of the garden from a shady protection.

Plates 2, 9, 10, 15, 24 and 31 are drawings of examples of garden houses.

The well with its pump, always located near the house, was sometimes covered with a structure that was very similar in design to a garden house. Plates 23 and 26 are measured drawings of well-houses.

Fence in front of the Jewett-Pattison House
Clarkson, N. Y.

Fence corner of 471 Mt. Hope Avenue and Clarissa Street
Rochester, N. Y.

Fragment of fence to Mrs. Judy MacFarland House on the Brockport-Bergen Rd.
Monroe County, N. Y.

Fence to Belcoda Cemetery
Monroe County, N. Y.

491 Mt. Hope Avenue
Rochester, N. Y.

Fence at Mr. Walter Coykendall
East Avon, N. Y.

Old fence posts "Christie Mill" Quarry Road
Near village of Caledonia, N. Y.

Fence to Henry Ridgely House
Rensselaerville, N. Y.

21

D. R. Sanders House, 39 South Street
Geneseo, N. Y.

Fence in Cooperstown, N. Y.

The "peacock" gate in fence on front of the Charles Waldrun House
Rensselaerville, N. Y.

Fence in front of the Chalres Waldrum House
Rensselaerville, N. Y.

23

Fence on the property of Mrs. Margaret Thompson
Claverack, N. Y.

Fence near Blossburg Penn.

Fence near "Sugar Loaf Mountain" near
Washington, D. C.

Fence in front of the Chase House
Annapolis, Maryland,

Fence in front of "Rosalie"
Natchez, Mississippi

Fence in front of the Topping - Reeves House
Litchfield, Conn.

Fence in front of the Richard Quay House
Litchfield, Conn.

Fence in Litchfield, Conn.

Fence in Litchfield, Conn.

Fence in front of one of the buildings of the Porter School
Farmington, Conn.

Gate to Cowles House
Farmington, Conn.

Fence in front of Mrs. Lucius Burch's home
Falls Village, Conn.

Fence in Woodbury, Conn.

Ropes Memorial, Salem, Mass.

Fence to Harry Thomas House
Salem, Mass.

Fence in front of the Pierce - Perry House
Newburyport, Mass.

Fence at 104 High Street,
Newburyport, Mass.

Garden House, in the Pierce - Perry Garden
Newburyport, Mass.

Fence in front of the Cushing – Bachman House
Newburyport, Mass.

Detail of Fence from Oliver House
142 Federal Street, Salem, Mass.

Fence to Ropes Memorial
Salem, Mass.

Fence to Dr. Moulton's House
Salem, Mass.

Grape Arbor, Ropes Memorial
Salem, Mass.

Fence in front of McDermoth House
#5 Chestnut Street, Salem, Mass.

36

Fence in Portsmouth, Mass.

Fence three miles south of
Hampton, N. H.

Fence to Museum at Portsmouth, N. H.

Fence in Portsmouth, N. H.

Fence at #160 Middle Road
Portsmouth, N. H.

Solid fence in front of garden to Larkin - Rich House, 180 Middle Street
Portsmouth, N. H.

Fence at #569 Middle Street
Portsmouth, N. H.

Fence at #546 Middle Street
Portsmouth, N. H.

Garden House, Goshen, Conn.

Garden House in the Garden of Dr. O'Dey
Country Club Lane, near Geneseo, N. Y.

Garden House, Bedfordshire, England

Well - House on West Main Street,
LeRoy, N. Y.

42

Garden House at Nathaniel White Residence,
Trumansburg, N. Y.

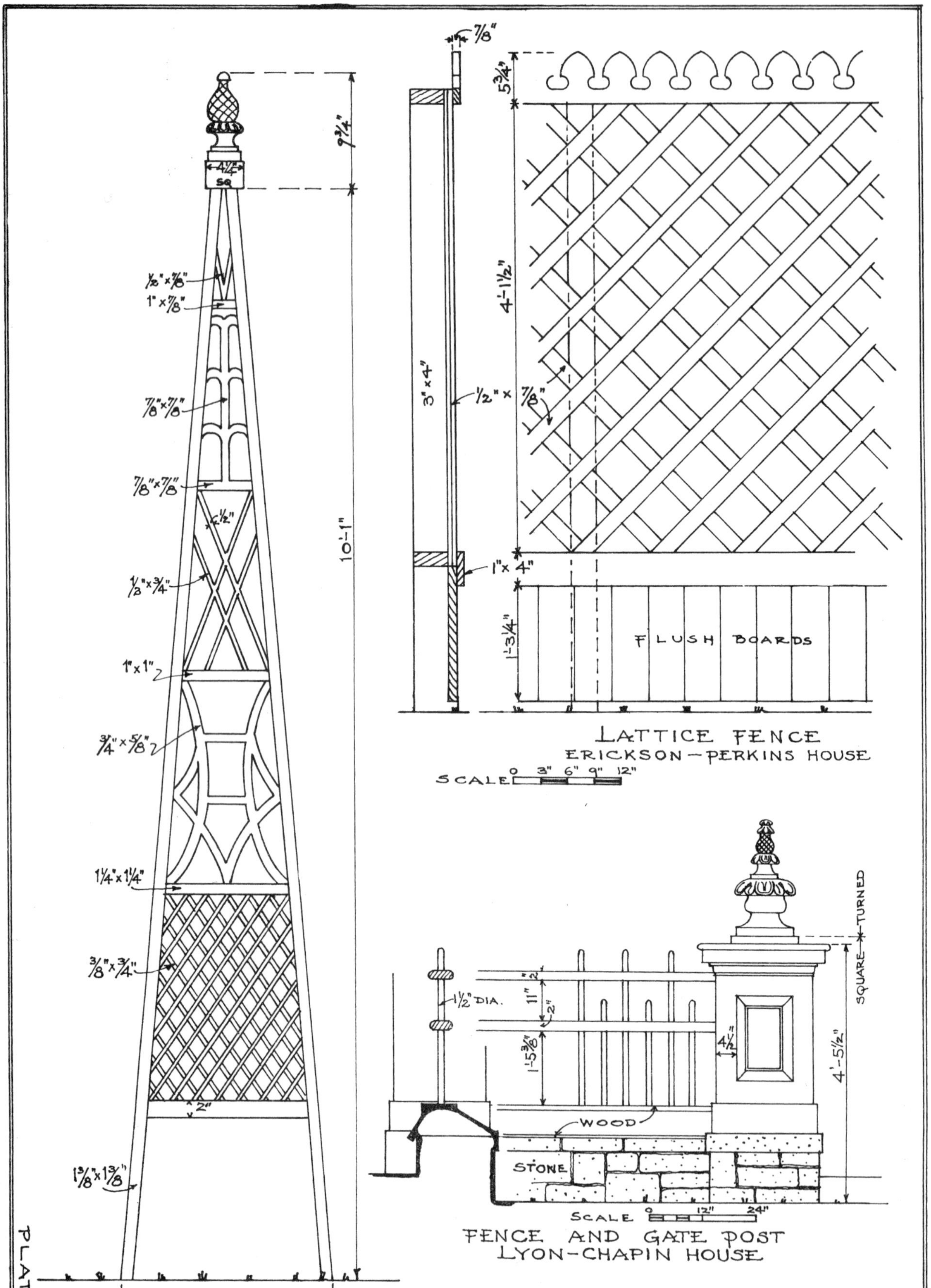
ROSE LATTICE
ERICKSON-PERKINS HOUSE
24½" SQUARE
10'-1"
9¾"
4½" SQ
½"x⅞"
1"x⅞"
⅞"x⅞"
⅞"x⅞"
1½"
⅓"x¾"
1"x1"
¾"x⅝"
1¼"x1¼"
⅜"x¾"
2"
1⅜"x1⅜"
PLATE 1
LATTICE FENCE
ERICKSON-PERKINS HOUSE
SCALE 0 3" 6" 9" 12"
⅞"
5¾"
4'-1½"
3"x4"
½"x⅞"
1"x4"
1'-3¼"
FLUSH BOARDS
FENCE AND GATE POST
LYON-CHAPIN HOUSE
SCALE 0 12" 24"
1½" DIA.
11"
2"
1'-5⅜"
4½"
4'-5½"
SQUARE
TURNED
WOOD
STONE
Measured And Drawn By
Carl F. Schmidt.
PLATE 1

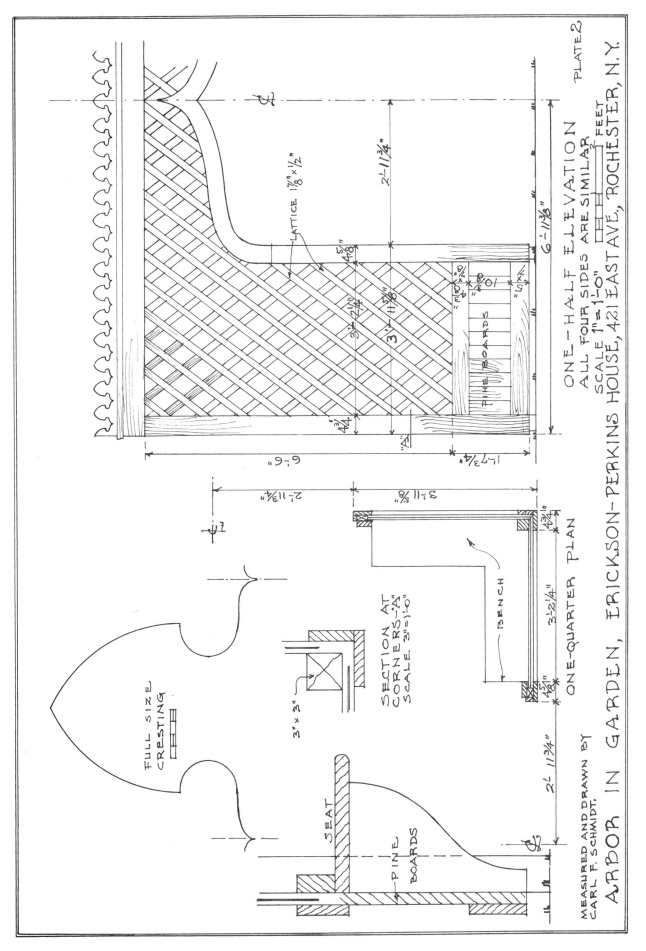

ONE-HALF ELEVATION
ALL FOUR SIDES ARE SIMILAR
SCALE 1"=1'-0"

LATTICE 1⅛" x ½"

PINE BOARDS

PLATE 2

FULL SIZE CRESTING

3" x 3"

SECTION AT CORNERS "A"
SCALE 3"=1'-0"

SEAT

PINE BOARDS

BENCH

ONE-QUARTER PLAN

MEASURED AND DRAWN BY
CARL F. SCHMIDT.

ARBOR IN GARDEN, ERICKSON-PERKINS HOUSE, 421 EAST AVE., ROCHESTER, N.Y.

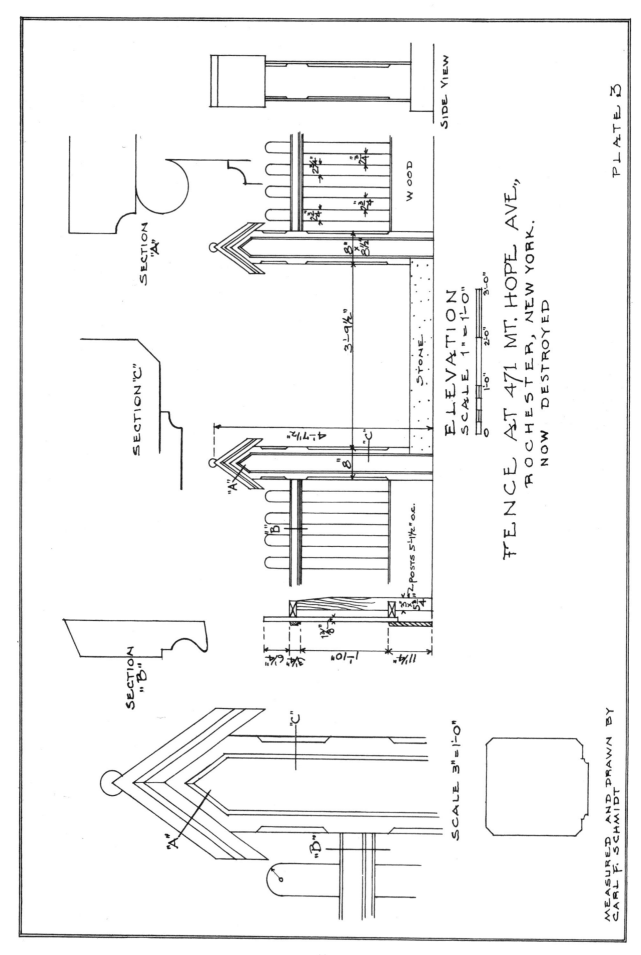

SECTION "A"

SECTION "C"

WOOD

$2\frac{3}{4}"$
$2\frac{3}{4}"$
$2\frac{3}{4}"$

$8" \times 8\frac{1}{2}"$

$3'-9\frac{1}{2}"$

STONE

ELEVATION
SCALE 1"=1'-0"

0   1'-0"   2'-0"   3'-0"

SIDE VIEW

$4'-1'\frac{1}{2}"$

"A"

"B"

"C"

$8"$

2 POSTS 5'-1$\frac{1}{2}$" O.C.

SECTION "B"

$5\frac{3}{4}" \times 3" \times 3"$

$1'\frac{7}{8}" \times 3"$

$6\frac{1}{4}"$
$4\frac{3}{4}"$
$3\frac{1}{4}"$

$1'-10"$

$11\frac{1}{4}"$

"C"

"A"

"B"

SCALE 3"=1'-0"

FENCE AT 471 MT. HOPE AVE.,
ROCHESTER, NEW YORK.
NOW DESTROYED

PLATE 3

MEASURED AND DRAWN BY
CARL F. SCHMIDT

46

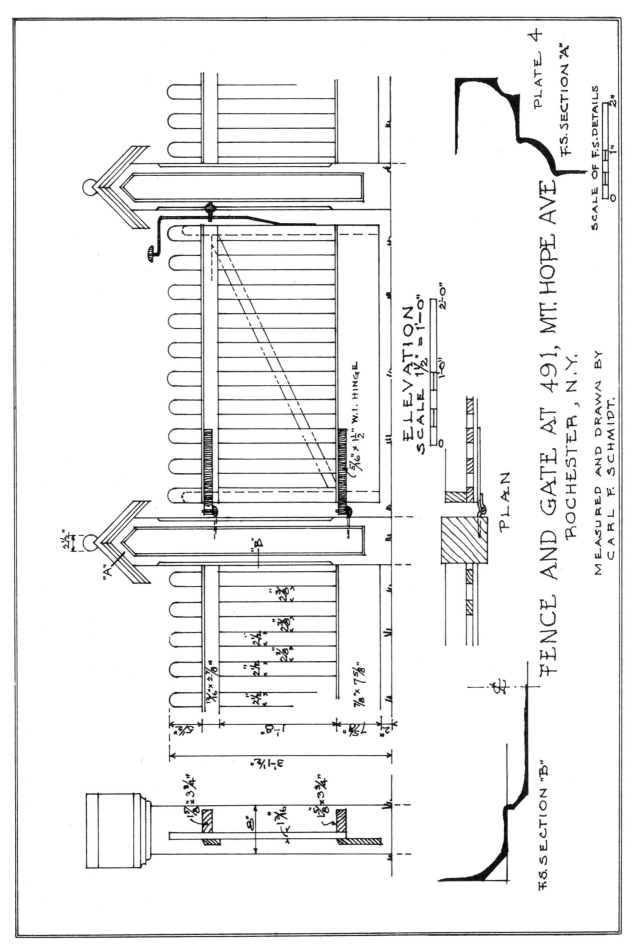

ELEVATION
SCALE 1½" = 1'-0"

PLAN

F.S. SECTION "B"

F.S. SECTION "A"

PLATE 4

SCALE OF F.S. DETAILS

FENCE AND GATE AT 491, MT. HOPE AVE.
ROCHESTER, N.Y.

MEASURED AND DRAWN BY
CARL F. SCHMIDT.

47

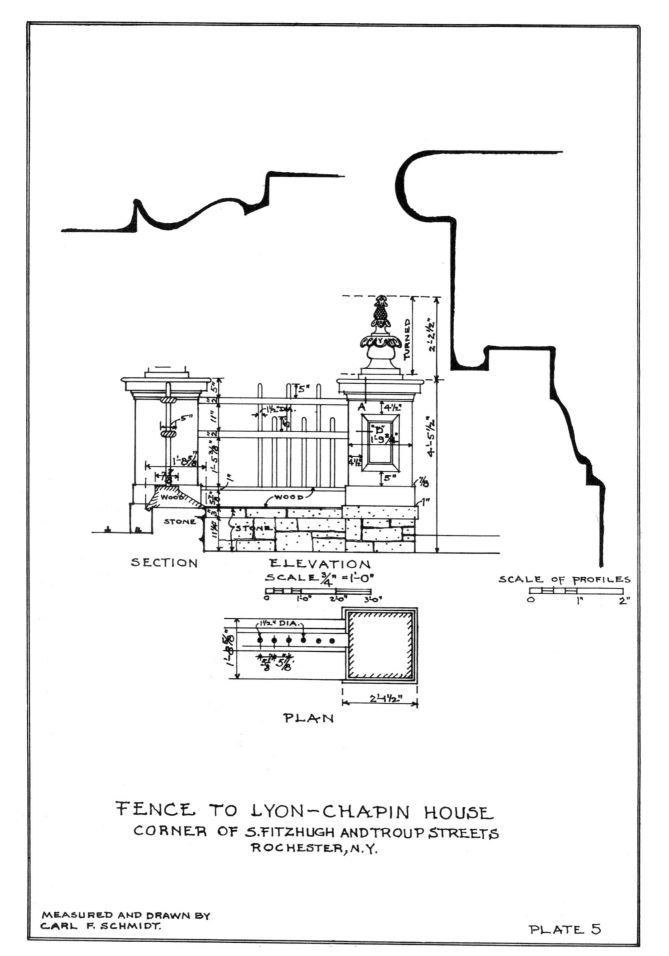

SECTION

ELEVATION
SCALE ¾" = 1'-0"

SCALE OF PROFILES

PLAN

FENCE TO LYON-CHAPIN HOUSE
CORNER OF S.FITZHUGH AND TROUP STREETS
ROCHESTER, N.Y.

MEASURED AND DRAWN BY
CARL F. SCHMIDT.

PLATE 5

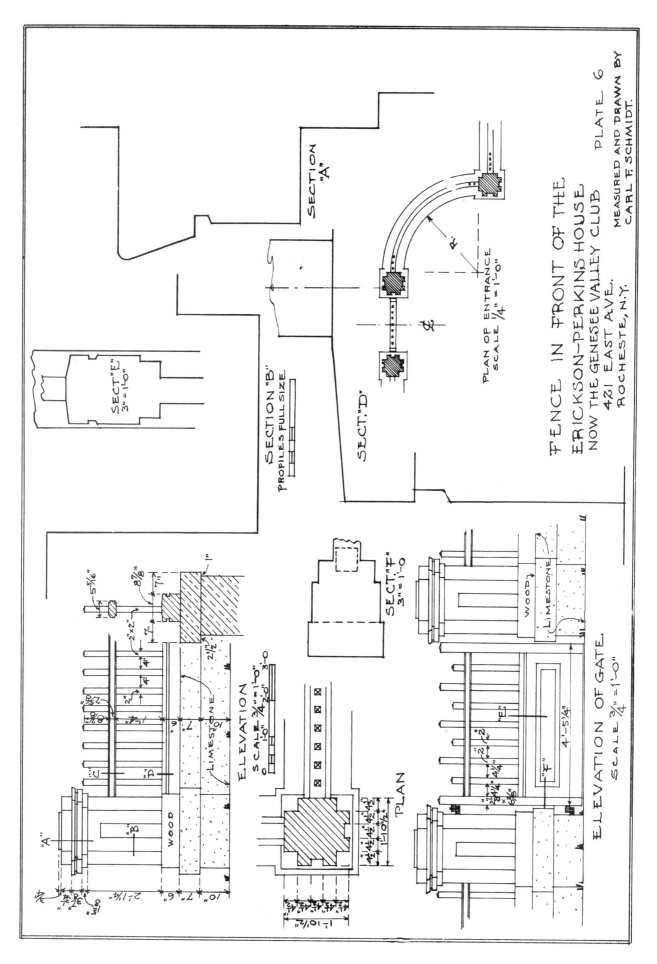

FENCE IN FRONT OF THE
ERICKSON-PERKINS HOUSE
NOW THE GENESEE VALLEY CLUB   PLATE 6
421 EAST AVE.
ROCHESTE, N.Y.

MEASURED AND DRAWN BY
CARL F. SCHMIDT.

SECTION "A"

SECT "E"
3"=1'-0"

SECTION "B"
PROFILES FULL SIZE

SECT."D"

PLAN OF ENTRANCE
SCALE 1/4" = 1'-0"

SECT."F"
3"=1'-0

ELEVATION
SCALE 3/4"=1'-0"

PLAN

ELEVATION OF GATE
SCALE 3/4" = 1'-0"

WOOD

LIMESTONE

WOOD

LIMESTONE

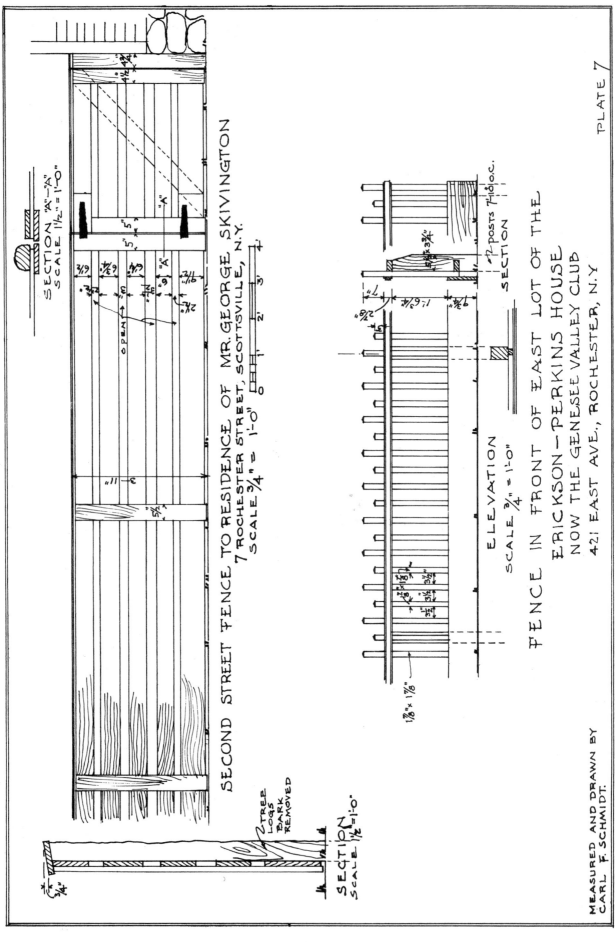

SECTION "A"—"A"
SCALE 1½" = 1'-0"

SECOND STREET FENCE TO RESIDENCE OF MR. GEORGE SKIVINGTON
7 ROCHESTER STREET, SCOTTSVILLE, N.Y.
SCALE ¾" = 1'-0"

SECTION
SCALE 1½" = 1'-0"

TREE LOGS BARK REMOVED

ELEVATION
SCALE ¾" = 1'-0"

SECTION

FENCE IN FRONT OF EAST LOT OF THE
ERICKSON—PERKINS HOUSE
NOW THE GENESEE VALLEY CLUB
421 EAST AVE., ROCHESTER, N.Y.

PLATE 7

MEASURED AND DRAWN BY
CARL F. SCHMIDT.

50

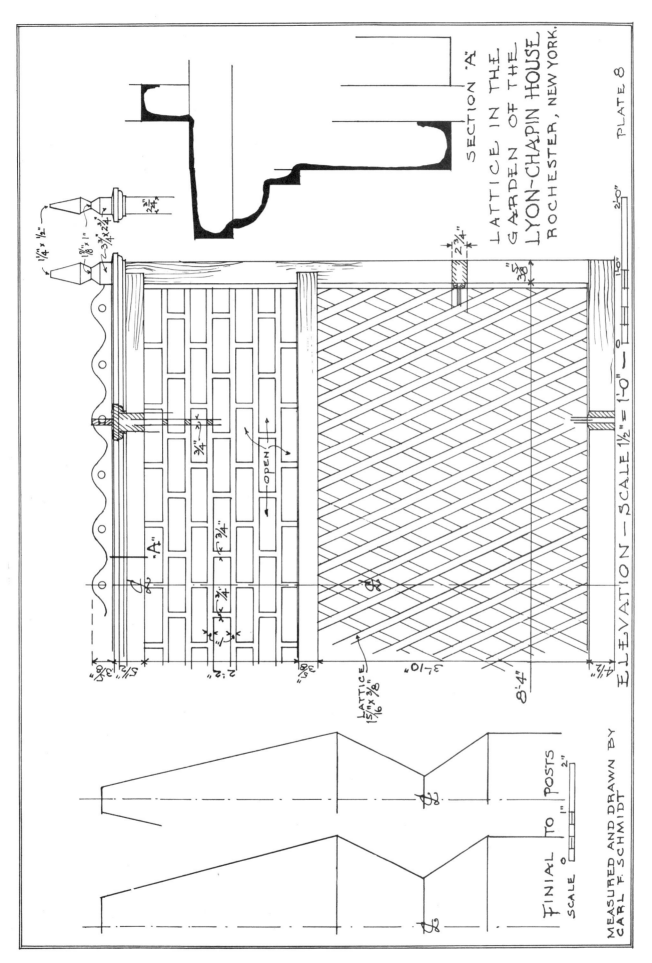

SECTION "A"

LATTICE IN THE
GARDEN OF THE
LYON-CHAPIN HOUSE.
ROCHESTER, NEW YORK.

PLATE 8

ELEVATION — SCALE 1½" = 1'-0"

FINIAL TO POSTS

SCALE 0 1" 2"

MEASURED AND DRAWN BY
CARL F. SCHMIDT

LATTICE 15⁄16" × ⅜"

8'-4"

3'-10"

"A"

3⁄4"

3⁄4"

OPEN

51

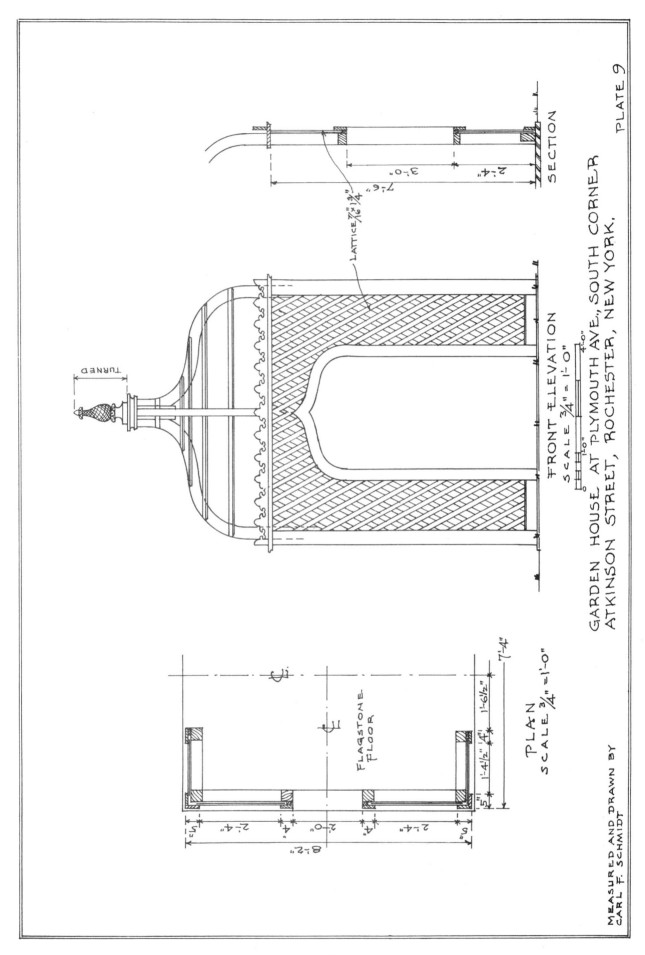

SECTION

PLATE 9

LATTICE 7/16" x 3/4"

7'-6"

3'-0"

2'-4"

TURNED

FRONT ELEVATION
SCALE 3/4" = 1'-0"

4'-0"

1'-0"

GARDEN HOUSE AT PLYMOUTH AVE., SOUTH CORNER
ATKINSON STREET, ROCHESTER, NEW YORK.

FLAGSTONE
FLOOR

7'-4"

1'-6½"

1'-4½" 4" 4" 4"

5"

2'-4"

2'-0"

2'-4"

5"

8'-2"

PLAN
SCALE 3/4" = 1'-0"

MEASURED AND DRAWN BY
CARL F. SCHMIDT

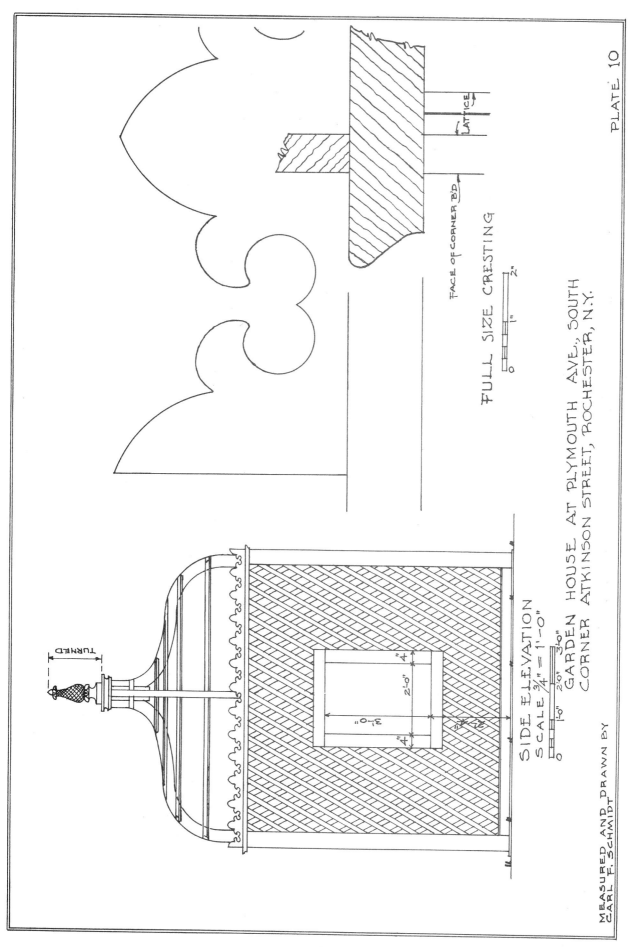

TURNED

LATTICE

FACE OF CORNER B'D

FULL SIZE CRESTING

0   1"   2"

SIDE ELEVATION
SCALE ¾" = 1'-0"

0   1'-0"   2'-0"   3'-0"

3'-0"

2'-0"

4"

4"

GARDEN HOUSE AT PLYMOUTH AVE., SOUTH
CORNER ATKINSON STREET, ROCHESTER, N.Y.

MEASURED AND DRAWN BY
CARL F. SCHMIDT

PLATE 10

53

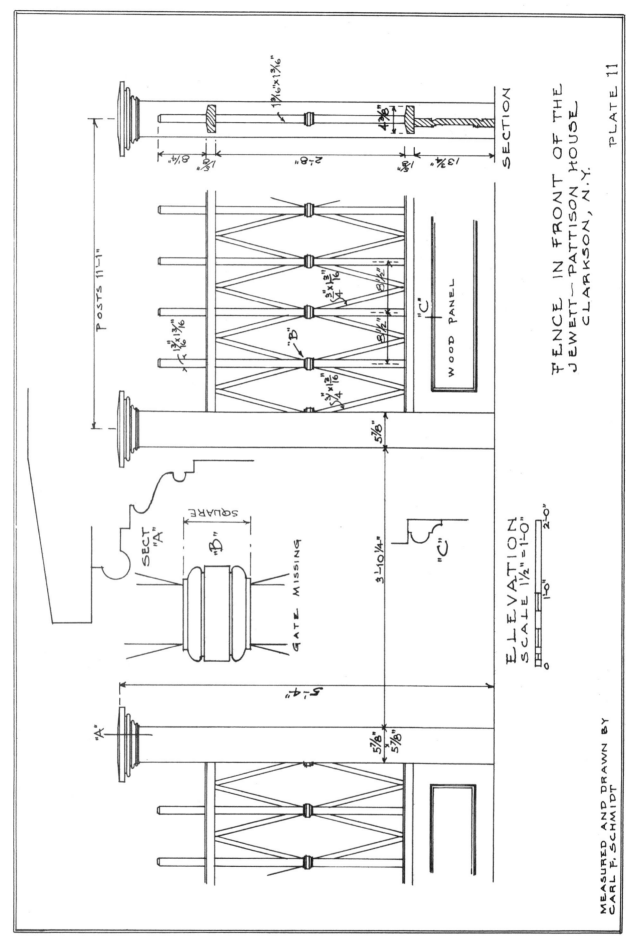

FENCE IN FRONT OF THE
JEWETT—PATTISON HOUSE
CLARKSON, N.Y.

PLATE 11

SECTION

POSTS 11'-1"

1¾"x1 3/16"

1 3/16"x1 3/16"

4⅜"

8¼"

⅝"

2'-8"

⅝"

13¾"

WOOD PANEL

"C"

"B"

5/4"x1 3/16"

5/4"x1 3/16"

8½"

8½"

5⅞"

SQUARE

SECT "A"

"B"

GATE MISSING

"C"

3'-10¼"

"A"

5'-4"

5⅞"

5⅞"

ELEVATION
SCALE 1½"=1'-0"

0   1'-0"   2'-0"

MEASURED AND DRAWN BY
CARL F. SCHMIDT

54

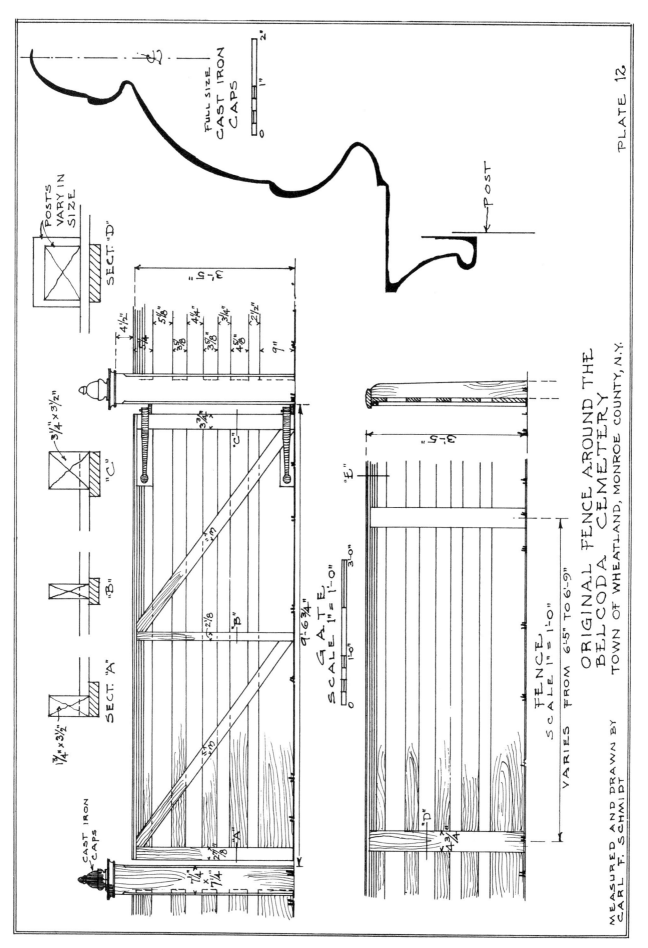

PLATE 12

FULL SIZE
CAST IRON
CAPS

POSTS VARY IN SIZE

SECT. "D"

POST

3'-1"

4½"
5⅝"
4¼"
3¾"
2½"
5¾"
3⅜"
3⅜"
4⅝"
9"

3'-5"

CAST IRON CAPS

3¾" × 3½"

SECT. "A"   "B"   "C"

1¾" × 3½"

3¾"

"C"

"B"

2⅝"

9'-6¾"

GATE
SCALE 1" = 1'-0"

"E"

3'-0"

7¼" × 7¼"

2⅞"   "A"

"D"

4¾"

FENCE
SCALE 1" = 1'-0"

VARIES FROM 6'-5" TO 6'-9"

ORIGINAL FENCE AROUND THE
BELCODA CEMETERY
TOWN OF WHEATLAND, MONROE COUNTY, N.Y.

MEASURED AND DRAWN BY
CARL F. SCHMIDT

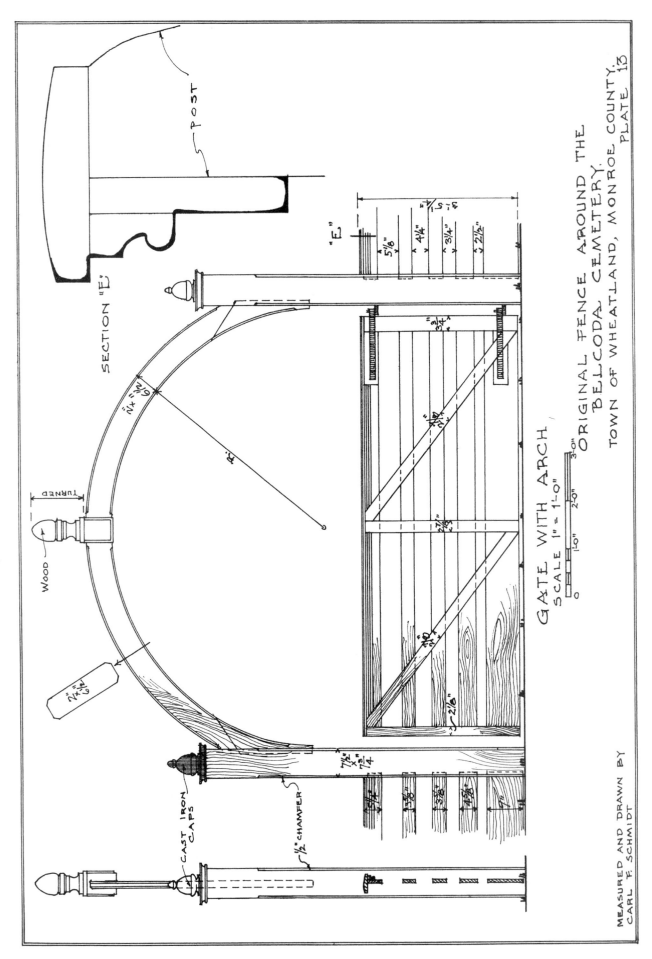

SECTION "E"

POST

"E"
5⅛"
4¼"
3¾"
2½"

TURNED
WOOD

6½"x½"

R

2¼"x½"

CAST IRON CAPS

½" CHAMFER

7½" x 7¼"

5¾"
1⅝"
3⅜"
4¾"
1"

3¾"

2⅞"
2⅜"

2½"

2½"
2¼"

GATE WITH ARCH
SCALE 1"=1'-0"

0   1'-0"   2'-0"   3'-0"

ORIGINAL FENCE AROUND THE
BELLCODA CEMETERY.
TOWN OF WHEATLAND, MONROE COUNTY.
PLATE 13

MEASURED AND DRAWN BY
CARL F. SCHMIDT

56

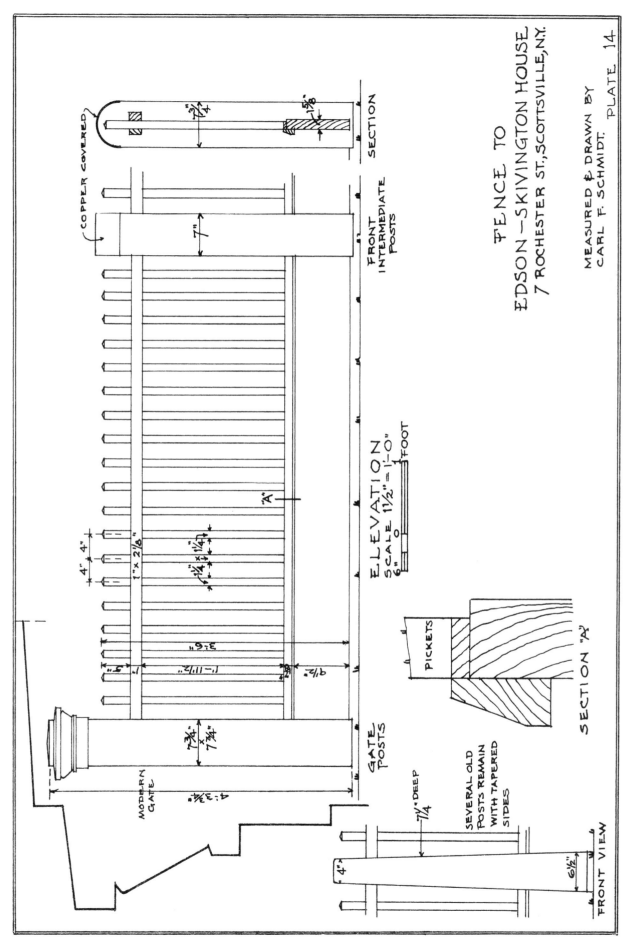

FENCE TO
EDSON—SKIVINGTON HOUSE
7 ROCHESTER ST., SCOTTSVILLE, N.Y.

MEASURED & DRAWN BY
CARL F. SCHMIDT.   PLATE 14

SECTION

COPPER COVERED

FRONT INTERMEDIATE POSTS

ELEVATION
SCALE 1½" = 1'-0"

SECTION "A"

PICKETS

GATE POSTS

MODERN GATE

SEVERAL OLD POSTS REMAIN WITH TAPERED SIDES

FRONT VIEW

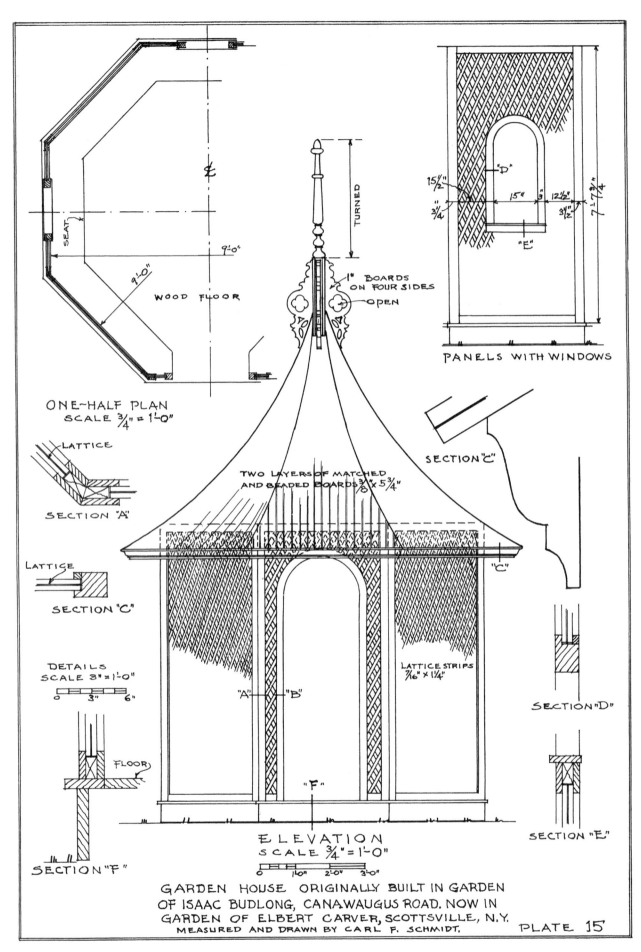

ONE-HALF PLAN
SCALE ¾" = 1'-0"

WOOD FLOOR

SEAT

9'-0"

9'-0"

TURNED

1" BOARDS
ON FOUR SIDES

OPEN

PANELS WITH WINDOWS

15½"

15"

3"

12½"

3¾"

7'-7¾"

¾"

"D"

"E"

LATTICE

SECTION "A"

SECTION "C"

LATTICE

SECTION "C"

TWO LAYERS OF MATCHED
AND BEADED BOARDS ⅜" x 5¾"

DETAILS
SCALE 3" = 1'-0"

0   3"   6"

"A"   "B"

"F"

LATTICE STRIPS
⁷⁄₁₆" x 1¼"

SECTION "D"

SECTION "E"

FLOOR

SECTION "F"

ELEVATION
SCALE ¾" = 1'-0"

0   1'-0"   2'-0"   3'-0"

GARDEN HOUSE ORIGINALLY BUILT IN GARDEN
OF ISAAC BUDLONG, CANAWAUGUS ROAD, NOW IN
GARDEN OF ELBERT CARVER, SCOTTSVILLE, N.Y.
MEASURED AND DRAWN BY CARL F. SCHMIDT.

PLATE 15

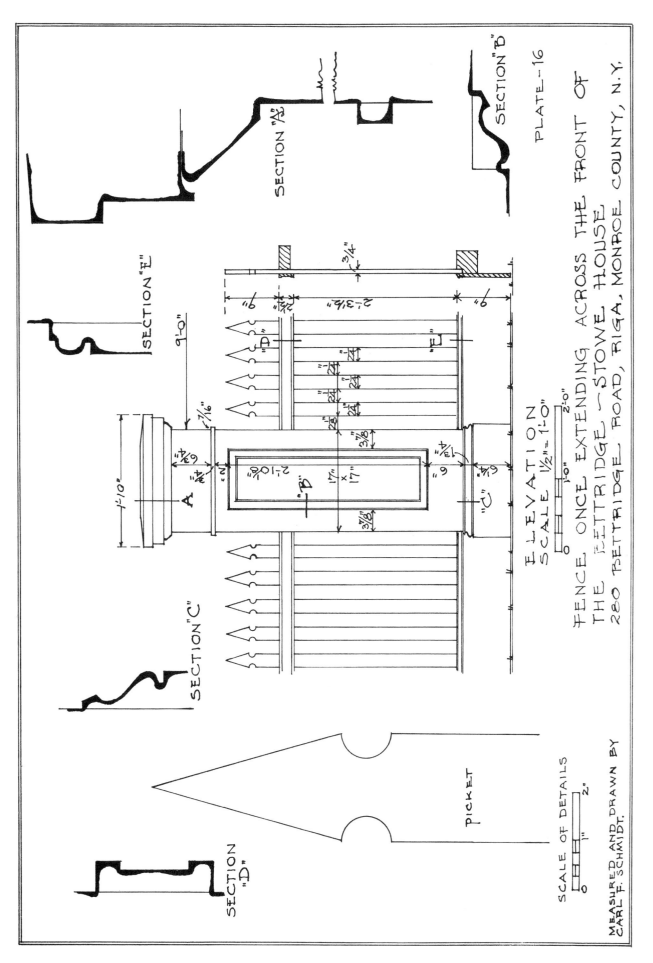

SECTION "A"

SECTION "B"

PLATE-16

SECTION "E"

ELEVATION
SCALE 1½" = 1'-0"

FENCE ONCE EXTENDING ACROSS THE FRONT OF
THE BETTRIDGE — STOWE HOUSE
280 BETTRIDGE ROAD, RIGA, MONROE COUNTY, N.Y.

SECTION "C"

PICKET

SECTION "D"

SCALE OF DETAILS

MEASURED AND DRAWN BY
CARL F. SCHMIDT.

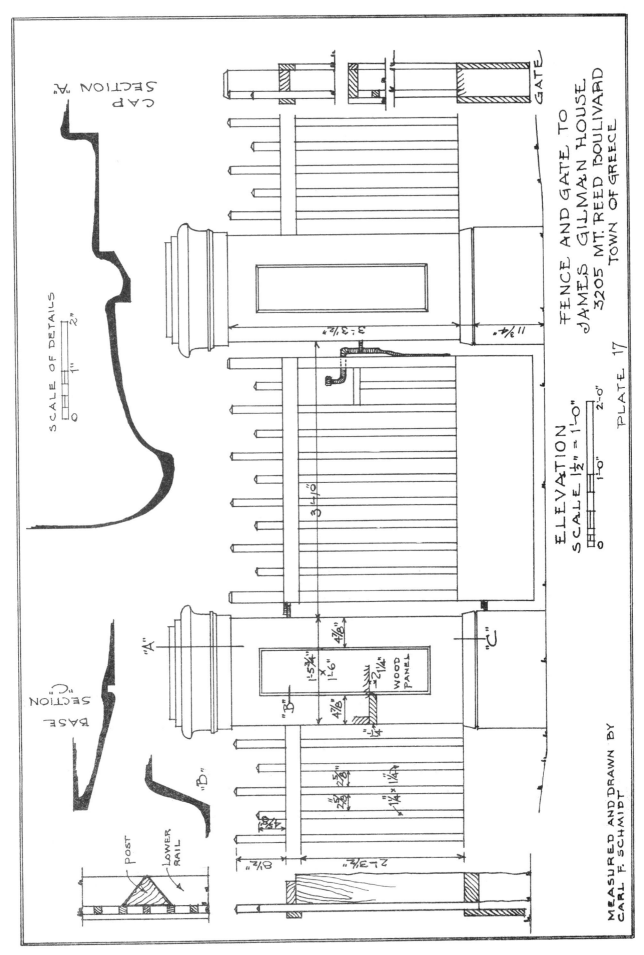

CAP SECTION "A"

SCALE OF DETAILS
0   1"   2"

BASE SECTION "C"

"A"

"B"

"C"

"D"

1'-5¾"
x
1'-6"

WOOD PANEL

2¼"

4⅞"

4⅞"

¼"

3'-3½"

11¾"

3'-0"

2⅝"
2⅝"

1¼" x 1¼"

4⅝"

8½"

2'-3½"

POST

LOWER RAIL

FENCE AND GATE TO
JAMES GILMAN HOUSE
3205 MT. REED BOULIVARD
TOWN OF GREECE

GATE

ELEVATION
SCALE 1½" = 1'-0"
0   1'-0"   2'-0"

PLATE 17

MEASURED AND DRAWN BY
CARL F. SCHMIDT

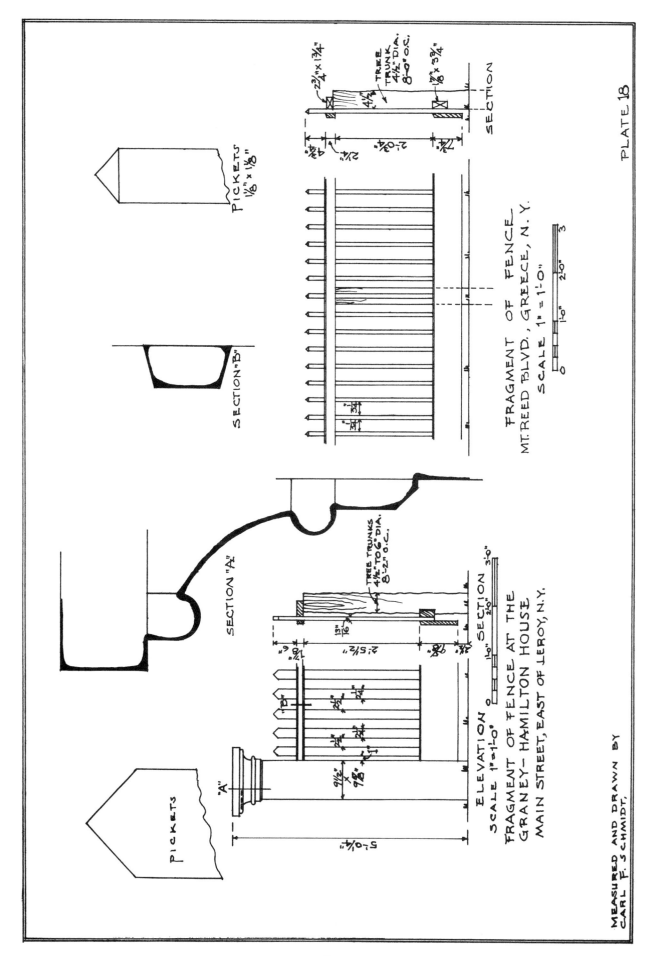

PICKETS
1⅛" x 1⅛"

SECTION "B"

TREE
TRUNK
4½" DIA.
8'-0" O.C.

SECTION

FRAGMENT OF FENCE
MT. REED BLVD., GREECE, N.Y.
SCALE 1" = 1'-0"

0   1'-0"   2'-0"   3

SECTION "A"

PICKETS

"A"

TREE TRUNKS
4½" TO 6" DIA.
8'-2" O.C.

ELEVATION
SCALE 1" = 1'-0"

0   1'-0"   2'-0"   3'-0"

SECTION

FRAGMENT OF FENCE AT THE
GRANEY - HAMILTON HOUSE
MAIN STREET, EAST OF LEROY, N.Y.

MEASURED AND DRAWN BY
CARL F. SCHMIDT.

PLATE 18

61

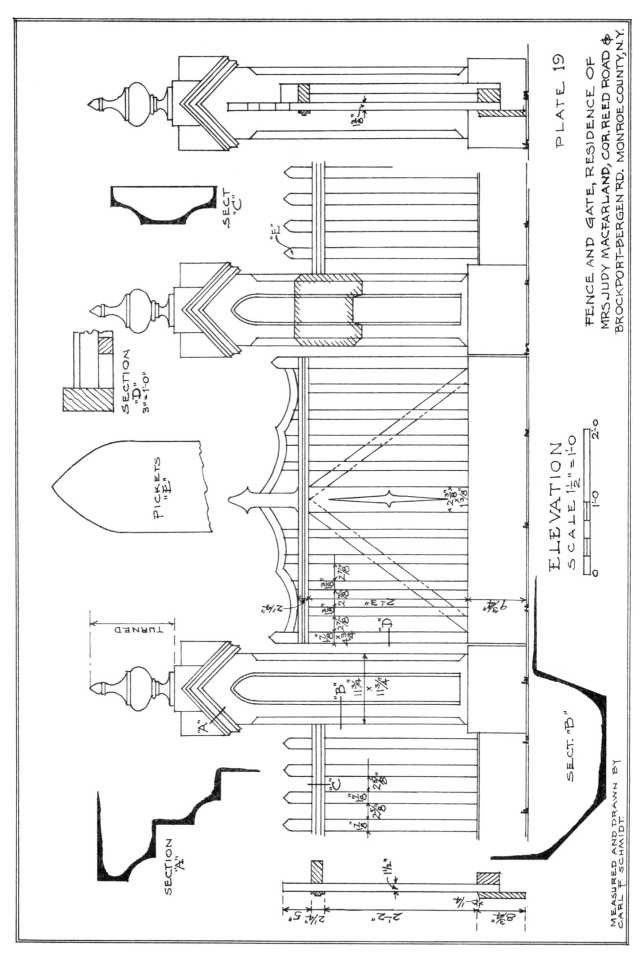

PLATE 19

FENCE AND GATE, RESIDENCE OF
MRS. JUDY MACFARLAND, COR. REED ROAD &
BROCKPORT-BERGEN RD. MONROE COUNTY, N.Y.

SECT "C"

SECTION "D"
3"=1'-0"

PICKETS "E"

"E"

SECTION "A"

TURNED

"A"

"B"
11¾"
x
11¾"

"C"

"D"

SECT. "D"

ELEVATION
SCALE 1½"=1'-0

0   1'-0   2'-0

MEASURED AND DRAWN BY
CARL F. SCHMIDT.

62

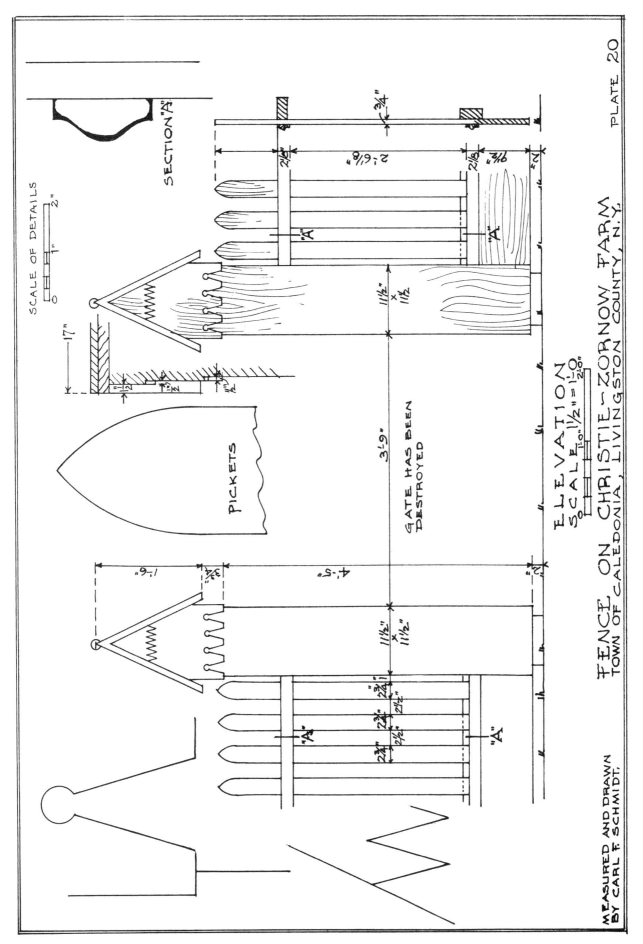

SECTION "A"

SCALE OF DETAILS
0 1" 2"

17"

PICKETS

GATE HAS BEEN DESTROYED

ELEVATION
SCALE 1½" = 1'-0"
1'-0"
2'-0"

FENCE ON CHRISTIE~ZORNOW FARM
TOWN OF CALEDONIA, LIVINGSTON COUNTY, N.Y.

MEASURED AND DRAWN
BY CARL F. SCHMIDT.

PLATE 20

63

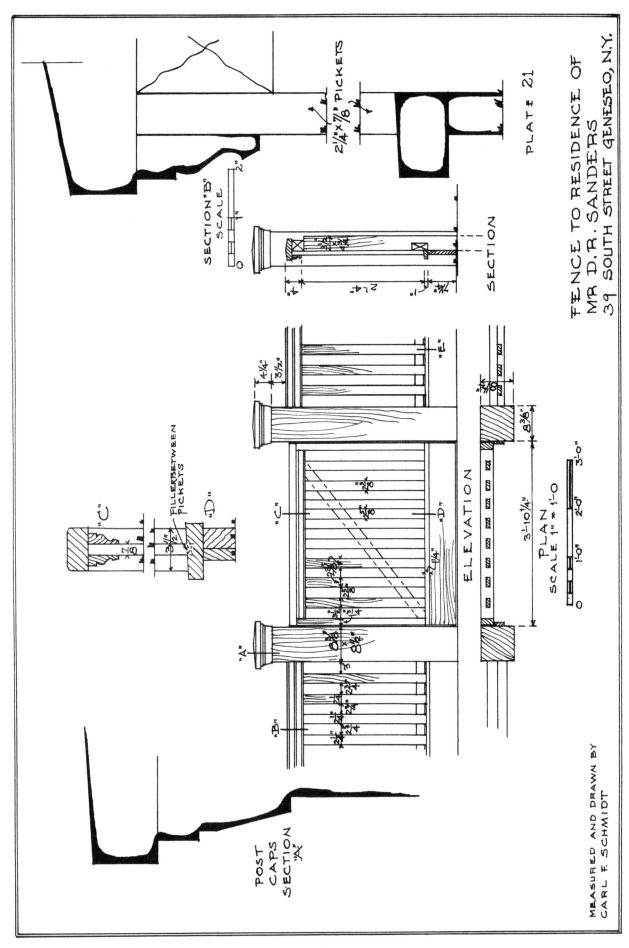

FENCE TO RESIDENCE OF
MR. D.R. SANDERS
39 SOUTH STREET GENESEO, N.Y.

PLATE 21

MEASURED AND DRAWN BY
CARL F. SCHMIDT

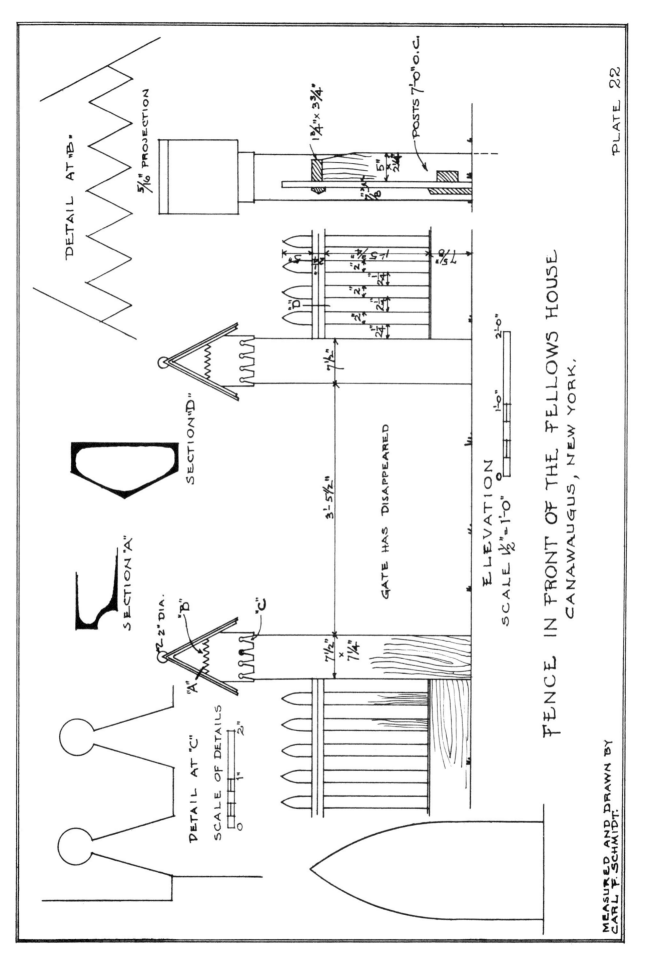

DETAIL AT "B"

5/16" PROJECTION

1¾" x 3¾"

POSTS 7'-0" O.C.

SECTION "D"

SECTION "A"

2.2" DIA.

DETAIL AT "C"

"A"
"B"
"C"

SCALE OF DETAILS

3'-5½"

GATE HAS DISAPPEARED

7½" x 7¼"

ELEVATION
SCALE ½"=1'-0"

FENCE IN FRONT OF THE FELLOWS HOUSE
CANAWAUGUS, NEW YORK.

MEASURED AND DRAWN BY
CARL F. SCHMIDT.

PLATE 22

65

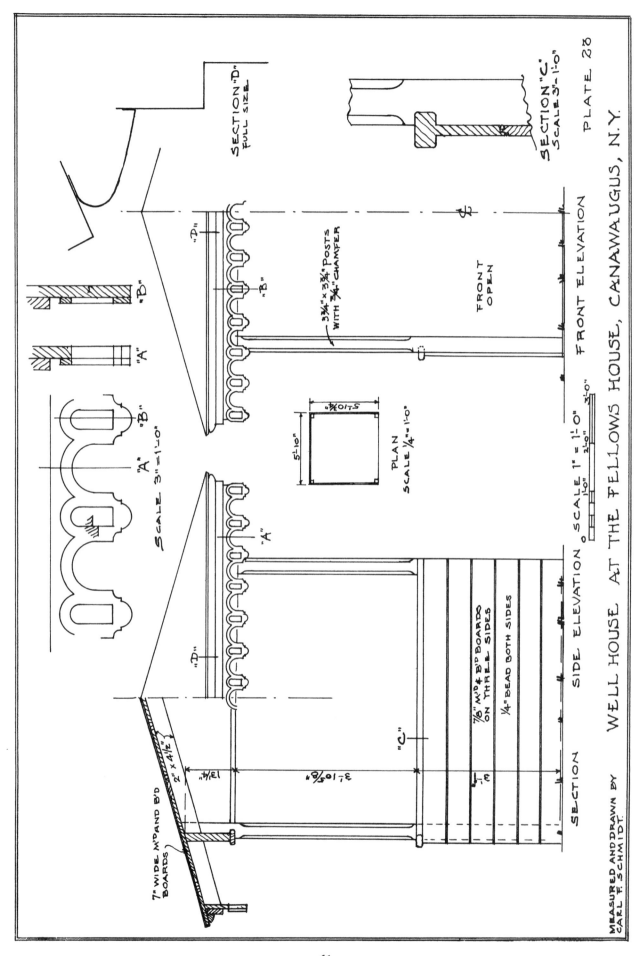

SECTION "D"
FULL SIZE

SECTION "C"
SCALE 3"=1'-0"

PLATE 28

"D"

"B"

3¾" × 3¾" POSTS
WITH ¾" CHAMFER

FRONT
OPEN

"B"

"A"

SCALE 3"=1'-0"

5'-10¾"

5'-10"

PLAN
SCALE ¼"=1'-0"

"A"

"D"

⅞" M'D & B'D BOARDS
ON THREE SIDES

¼" BEAD BOTH SIDES

"C"

2" × 4½"

13¾"

3'-10⅝"

7" WIDE M'D AND B'D
BOARDS

SECTION   SIDE ELEVATION   SCALE 1" = 1'-0"   FRONT ELEVATION

WELL HOUSE AT THE FELLOWS HOUSE, CANAWAUGUS, N.Y.

MEASURED AND DRAWN BY
CARL F. SCHMIDT.

66

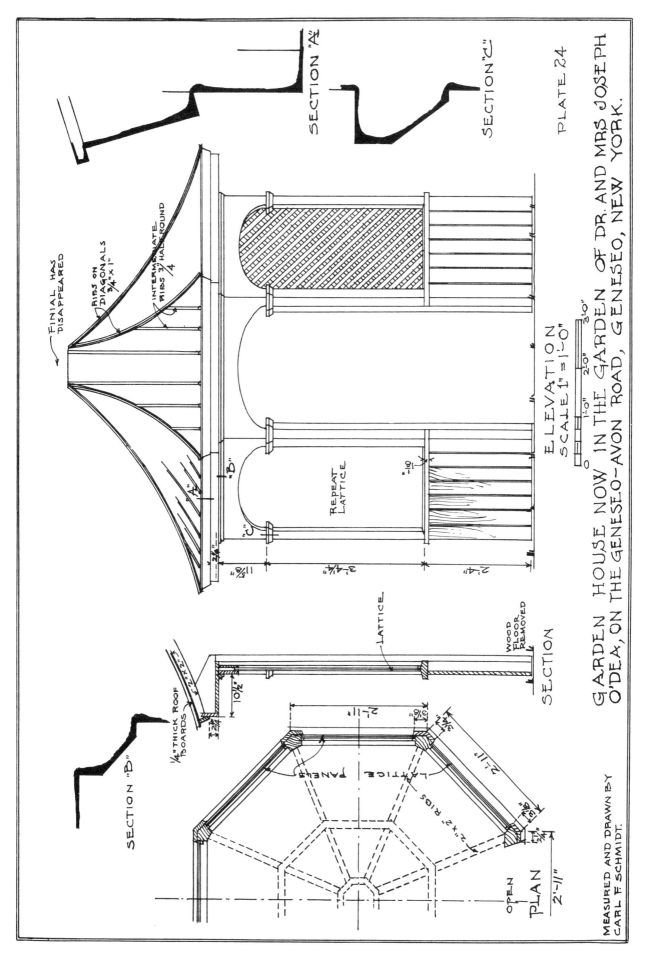

SECTION "A"

SECTION "C"

PLATE 24

FINIAL HAS DISAPPEARED

RIBS ON DIAGONALS 3/4" x 1"

INTERMEDIATE RIBS 3/4" HALF ROUND

"B"

"A"

"C"

REPEAT LATTICE

1'-10"

2 1/4"

11 5/8"

3'-4 1/4"

2 1/4"

ELEVATION
SCALE 1" = 1'-0"

0   1'-0"   2'-0"   3'-0"

SECTION "B"

1/4" THICK ROOF BOARDS

2" x 2"

10 1/2"

1 2 1/4"

LATTICE

WOOD FLOOR REMOVED

SECTION

2'-11"

1 5/8"

LATTICE PANELS

2'-11"

2" x 2" RIBS

OPEN

PLAN
2'-11"

GARDEN HOUSE NOW IN THE GARDEN OF DR. AND MRS JOSEPH
O'DEA, ON THE GENESEO-AVON ROAD, GENESEO, NEW YORK.

MEASURED AND DRAWN BY
CARL F. SCHMIDT.

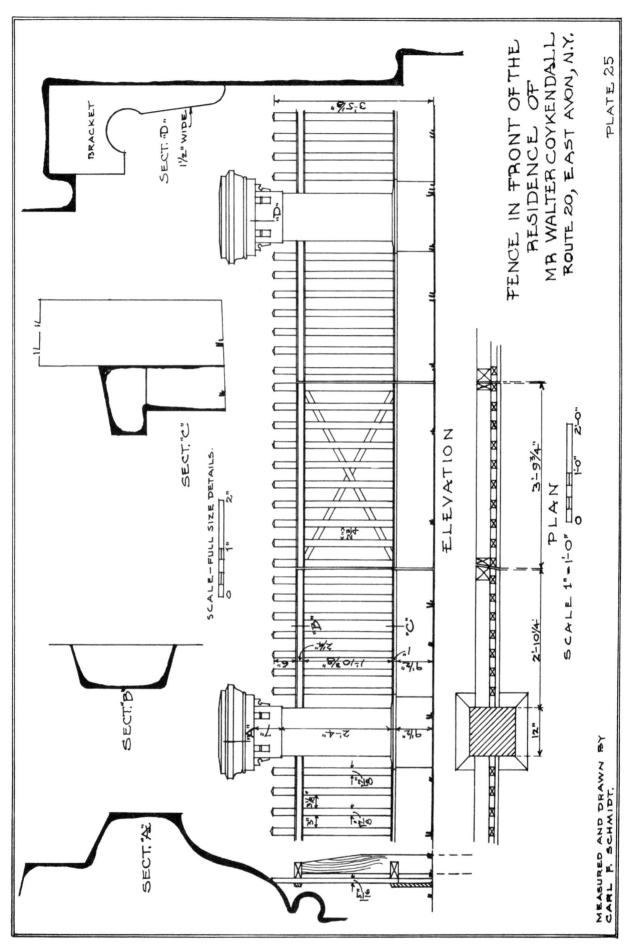

BRACKET

SECT. "D"
1½" WIDE.

SECT. "C"

SCALE–FULL SIZE DETAILS.
0 1" 2"

SECT. "B"

SECT. "A"

3'-5⅝"

"D"

ELEVATION

"D"

"C"

2'-10¼"

3'-9¾"

PLAN
SCALE 1"=1'-0"
0 1'-0" 2'-0"

12"

2'-4"

FENCE IN FRONT OF THE
RESIDENCE OF
MR WALTER COYKENDALL
ROUTE 20, EAST AVON, N.Y.

PLATE 25

MEASURED AND DRAWN BY
CARL F. SCHMIDT.

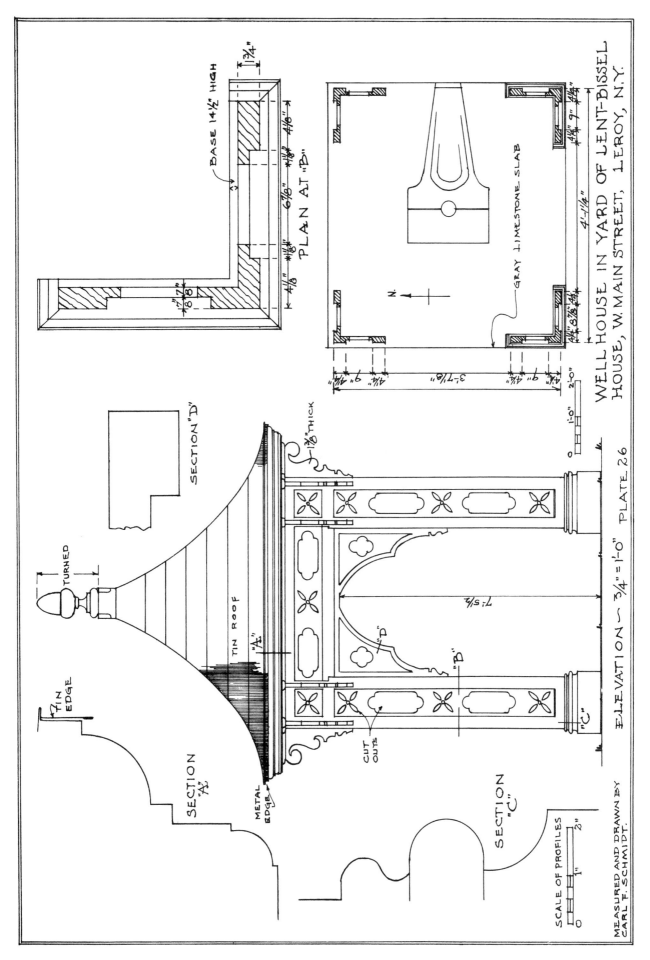

BASE 14½ HIGH

1¾"

4⅛"
4⅛"
6⅛"
1⅛"
1⅛"
4⅛"
7"
7"
8"

PLAN AT "B"

9" 4¼" 4¼" 9"

4'-1¼"
4¼" 9" 8½" 4¼"

N.

GRAY LIMESTONE SLAB

3'-7⅞"

4¼" 9" 4¼"

2'-0"
1'-0"
0

1⅛"THICK

SECTION "D"

TURNED

TIN EDGE

TIN ROOF

"A"

SECTION "A"

METAL EDGE

"D"

7'-5¾"

"B"

"C"

CUT OUTS

SECTION "C"

SCALE OF PROFILES
0 1" 2"

WELL HOUSE IN YARD OF LENT-BISSEL HOUSE, W. MAIN STREET, LEROY, N.Y.

ELEVATION ~ ¾" = 1'-0"   PLATE 26

MEASURED AND DRAWN BY
CARL F. SCHMIDT.

69

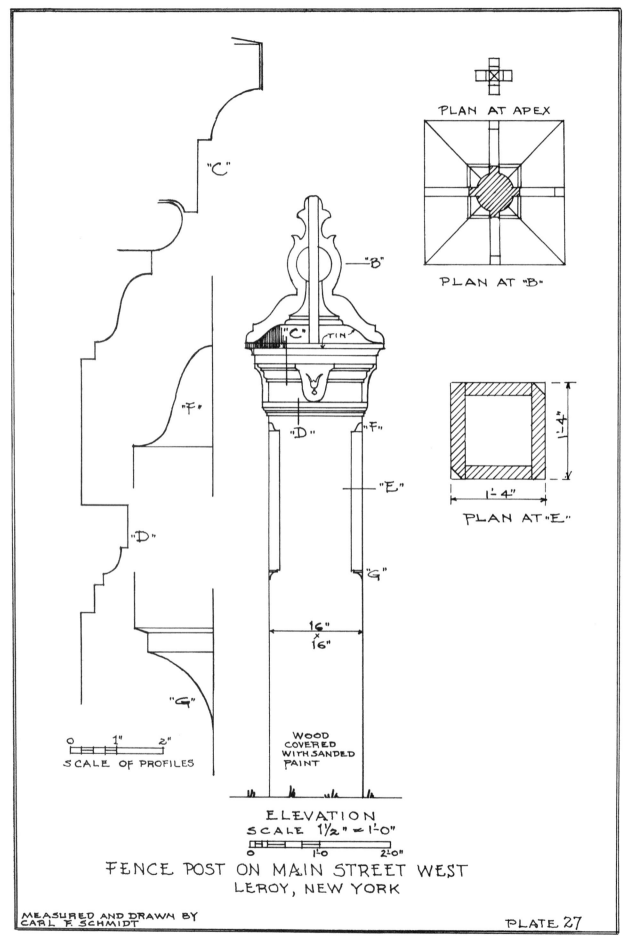

"C"

"B"

"C"

TIN

"D"

"F"

"E"

"D"

"G"

16"
x
16"

"F"

"G"

PLAN AT APEX

PLAN AT "B"

1'-4"

1'-4"

PLAN AT "E"

0   1"   2"

SCALE OF PROFILES

WOOD
COVERED
WITH SANDED
PAINT

ELEVATION
SCALE 1½" = 1'-0"

0   1'-0   2'-0"

FENCE POST ON MAIN STREET WEST
LEROY, NEW YORK

MEASURED AND DRAWN BY
CARL F. SCHMIDT

PLATE 27

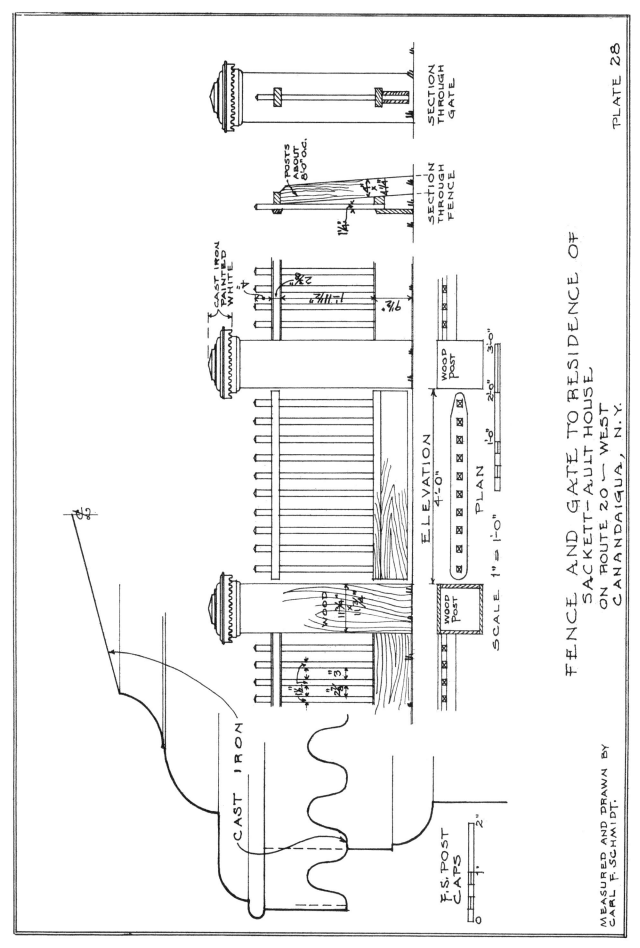

SECTION THROUGH GATE

SECTION THROUGH FENCE

POSTS ABOUT 8'-0" O.C.

1¼"

CAST IRON PAINTED WHITE

2⅜"

1'-11½"

³/₁₆"

WOOD POST

3'-0"

2'-0"

1'-0"

ELEVATION
4'-0"

PLAN

SCALE 1" = 1'-0"

WOOD POST

WOOD

CAST IRON

F.S. POST CAPS

FENCE AND GATE TO RESIDENCE OF
SACKETT—AULT HOUSE
ON ROUTE 20 — WEST
CANANDAIGUA, N.Y.

MEASURED AND DRAWN BY
CARL F. SCHMIDT.

PLATE 28

71

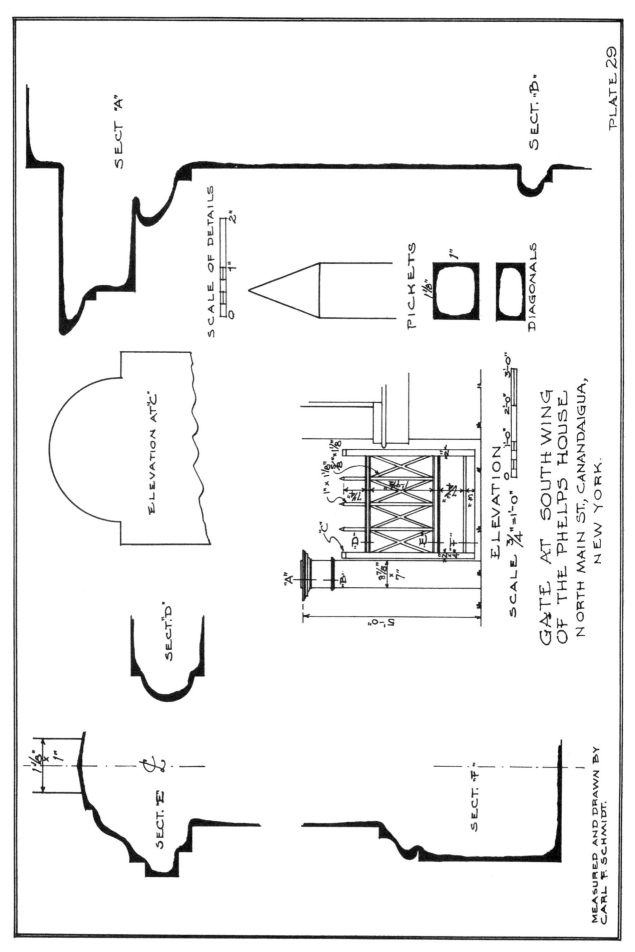

SECT "A"

SECT "B"

SCALE OF DETAILS

PICKETS

DIAGONALS

ELEVATION AT "C"

SECT "D"

SECT "E"

SECT "F"

ELEVATION
SCALE ¾"=1'-0"

GATE AT SOUTH WING
OF THE PHELPS HOUSE
NORTH MAIN ST., CANANDAIGUA,
NEW YORK.

MEASURED AND DRAWN BY
CARL F. SCHMIDT.

PLATE 29

72

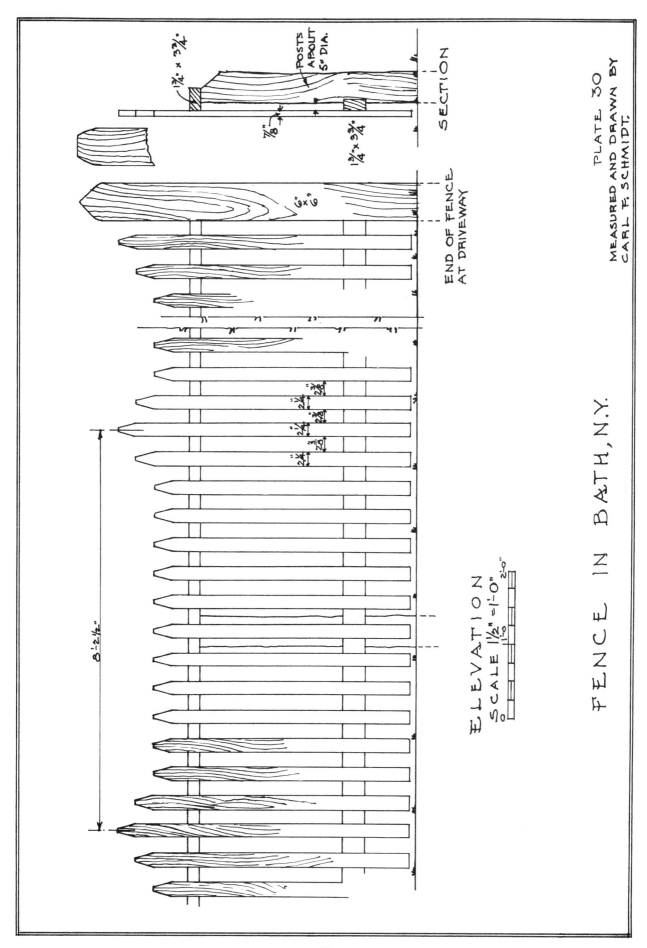

SECTION

POSTS ABOUT 5" DIA.

1¾" × 3¾"

⅞"

1¾" × 3¾"

6" × 6"

END OF FENCE
AT DRIVEWAY

8'-2½"

2¼" 2⅜"
2¼" 2⅜"
2¼" 2⅜"
2¼" 2⅜"

ELEVATION
SCALE 1½" = 1'-0"

FENCE IN BATH, N.Y.

PLATE 30

MEASURED AND DRAWN BY
CARL F. SCHMIDT.

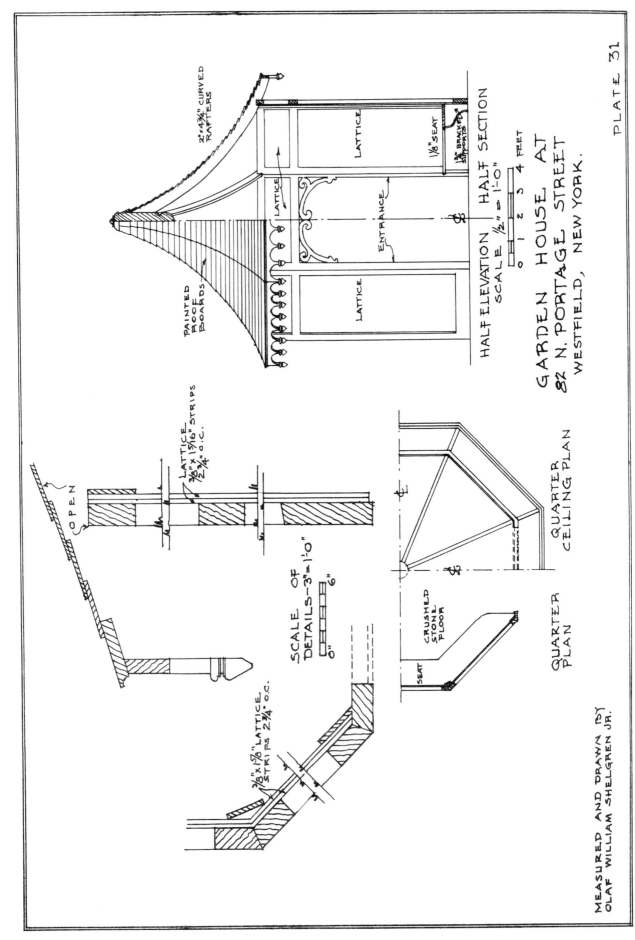

2"x4¾" CURVED RAFTERS

LATTICE

LATTICE

LATTICE

LATTICE

1⅛" SEAT

1⅜" BRACKET SUPPORTS

ENTRANCE

PAINTED ROOF BOARDS

HALF ELEVATION   HALF SECTION
SCALE ½" = 1'-0"

0 1 2 3 4 FEET

GARDEN HOUSE AT
82 N. PORTAGE STREET
WESTFIELD, NEW YORK.

PLATE 31

OPEN

LATTICE
⅜" x 1⁵⁄₁₆" STRIPS
2¾" O.C.

SCALE OF
DETAILS—3"=1'-0"

0"   6"

⅜" x 1⅝" LATTICE
STRIPS 2¾" O.C.

QUARTER
CEILING PLAN

CRUSHED
STONE
FLOOR

SEAT

QUARTER
PLAN

MEASURED AND DRAWN BY
OLAF WILLIAM SHELGREN JR.

74

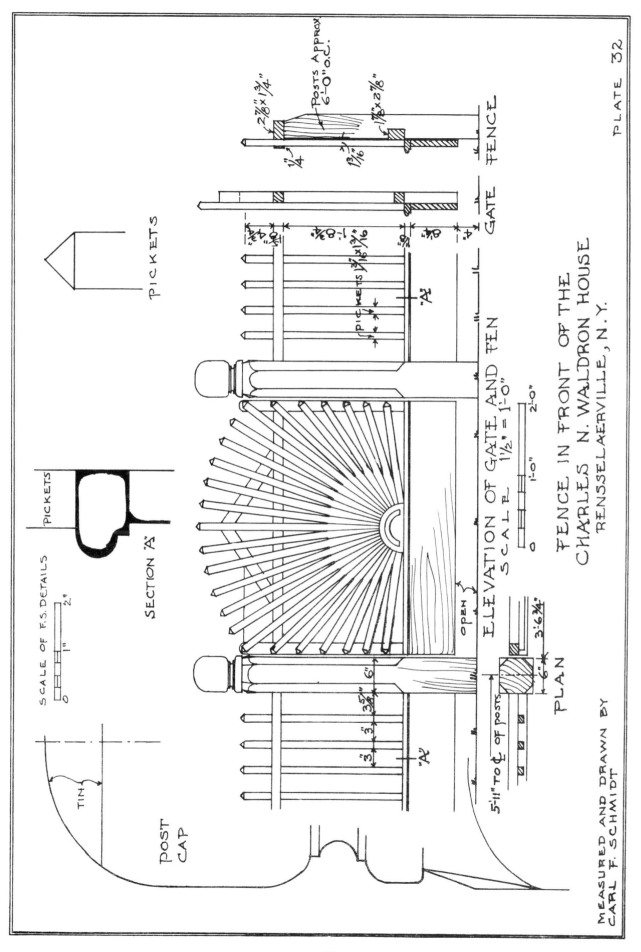

PICKETS

SECTION "A"

PICKETS

SCALE OF F.S. DETAILS
0   1"   2"

POST CAP

TIN

PICKETS

Posts Approx
6'-0" o.c.

2⅞" x 1¾"

1⅞" x 2⅛"

¼"

1 3/16"

GATE   FENCE

PICKETS 1³⁄₁₆ x 1 ³/₁₆"

"A"

"A"

3" 3" 3⅜" 3⅝" 6"

OPEN

ELEVATION OF GATE AND FEN
SCALE 1½" = 1'-0"

0   1'-0"   2'-0"

3'-6¾"

6"

5'-11" TO ℄ OF POSTS

PLAN

FENCE IN FRONT OF THE
CHARLES N. WALDRON HOUSE
RENSSELAERVILLE, N.Y.

MEASURED AND DRAWN BY
CARL F. SCHMIDT

PLATE   32

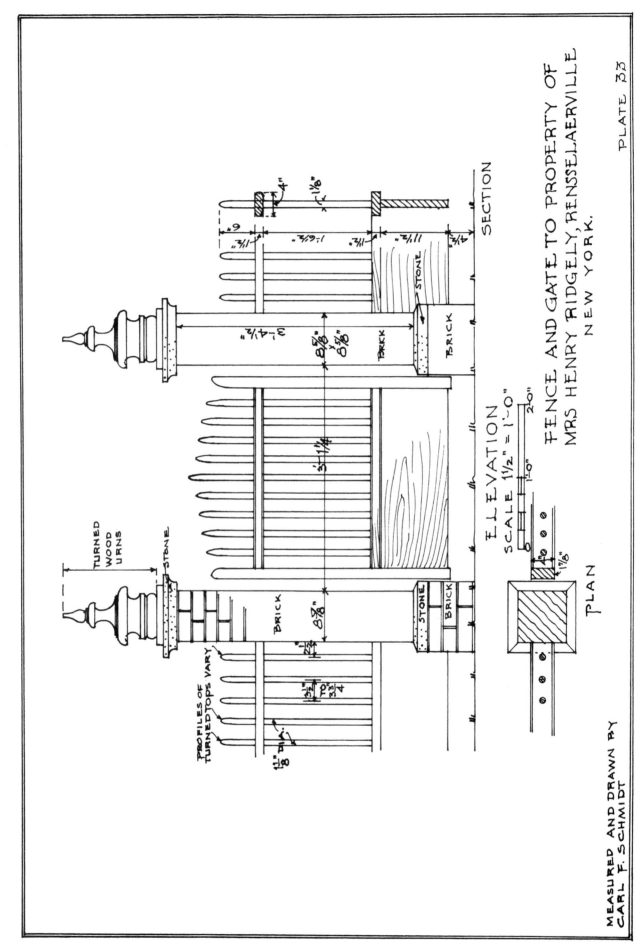

TURNED WOOD URNS

PROFILES OF TURNED TOPS VARY

1 1/2" DIA.

1 1/2" TO 3 3/4"

STONE

BRICK

BRICK

STONE

8 7/8"

3'-1 1/4"

8 5/8" X 8 5/8"

3'-4 1/2"

BRICK

BRICK

STONE

SECTION

6"

1 3/4"

1'-9 3/4"

1 3/4"

11 1/2"

1 1/4"

4"

1 1/8"

1 7/8"

1'-0"

2'-0"

ELEVATION
SCALE 1 1/2" = 1'-0"

PLAN

FENCE AND GATE TO PROPERTY OF
MRS HENRY RIDGELY, RENSSELAERVILLE
NEW YORK.

PLATE 33

MEASURED AND DRAWN BY
CARL F. SCHMIDT

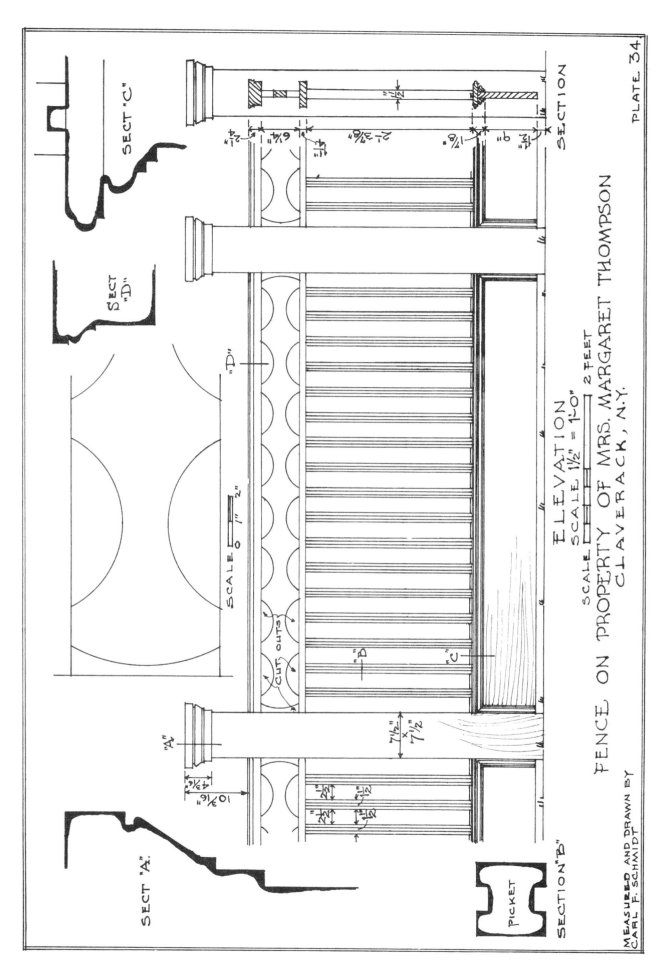

SECT "C"

SECT "D"

SECT "A".

SCALE 0 1" 2"

CUT OUTS

SECTION "B"

PICKET

SECTION

2½"
6¼"
1¼"
2'-3⅜"
1⅛"
9"
1½"
½"

4¾"
10³/₁₆"

"A"
"D"
"B"
"C"

7½" x 7½"

2½"
2½"
1½"
1½"

ELEVATION
SCALE 1½" = 1'-0"

SCALE 0 1 2 FEET

FENCE ON PROPERTY OF MRS. MARGARET THOMPSON
CLAVERACK, N.Y.

MEASURED AND DRAWN BY
CARL F. SCHMIDT

PLATE 34

77

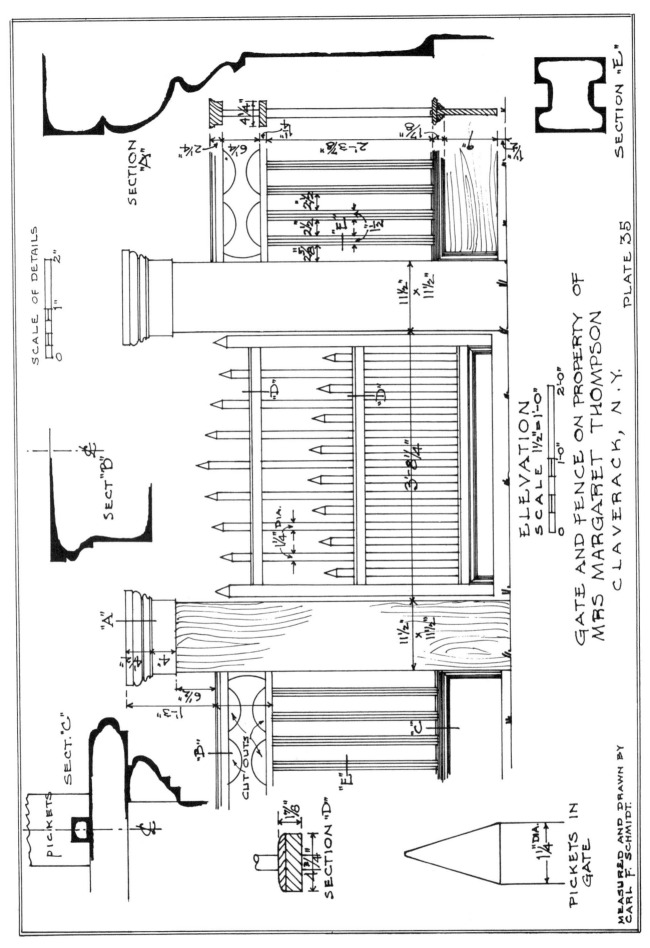

SECTION "E"

SECTION "A"

SCALE OF DETAILS

0   1"   2"

SECT "B"

SECT. "C"

PICKETS

ELEVATION
SCALE 1½"=1'-0"

0   1'-0"   2'-0"

GATE AND FENCE ON PROPERTY OF
MRS MARGARET THOMPSON
CLAVERACK, N.Y.

PLATE 35

SECTION "D"

PICKETS IN GATE

MEASURED AND DRAWN BY
CARL F. SCHMIDT.

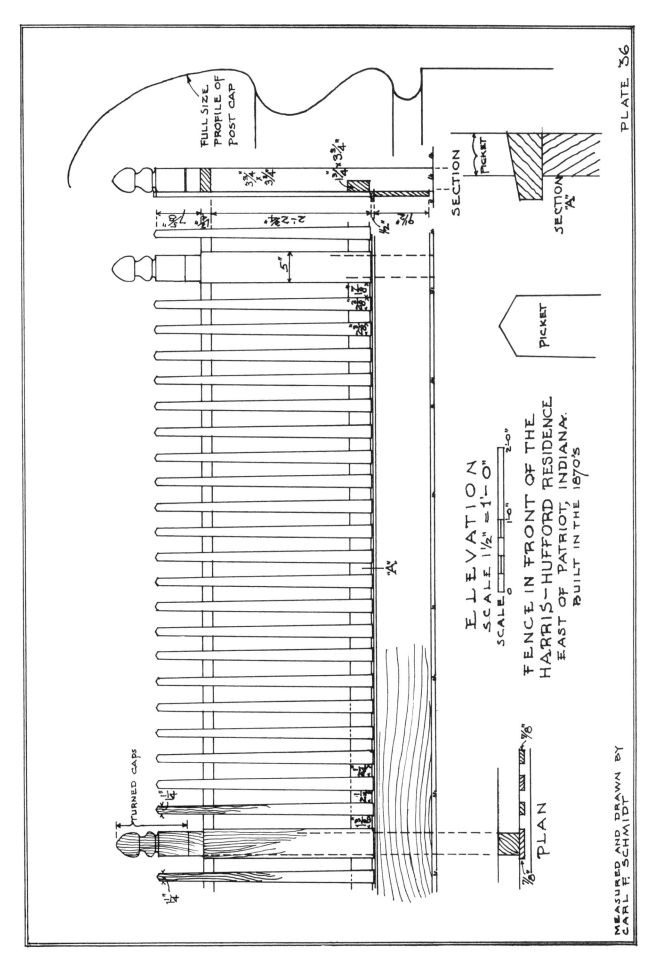

FULL SIZE PROFILE OF POST CAP

3¾"
x
¾

¼" x 3¾"

SECTION

SECTION "A"

PICKET

PICKET

7/8"
⅝
2'-2¾"

5"

2⅜
2⅜ x ⅝

2⅜"

"A"

TURNED CAPS

1¼"

1¾"
⅝

2"

ELEVATION
SCALE 1½" = 1'-0"

SCALE 0   1'-0"   2'-0"

FENCE IN FRONT OF THE
HARRIS—HUFFORD RESIDENCE
EAST OF PATRIOT, INDIANA.
BUILT IN THE 1870's

PLAN

⅞"

⅞"

1¼"

MEASURED AND DRAWN BY
CARL F. SCHMIDT

PLATE 36

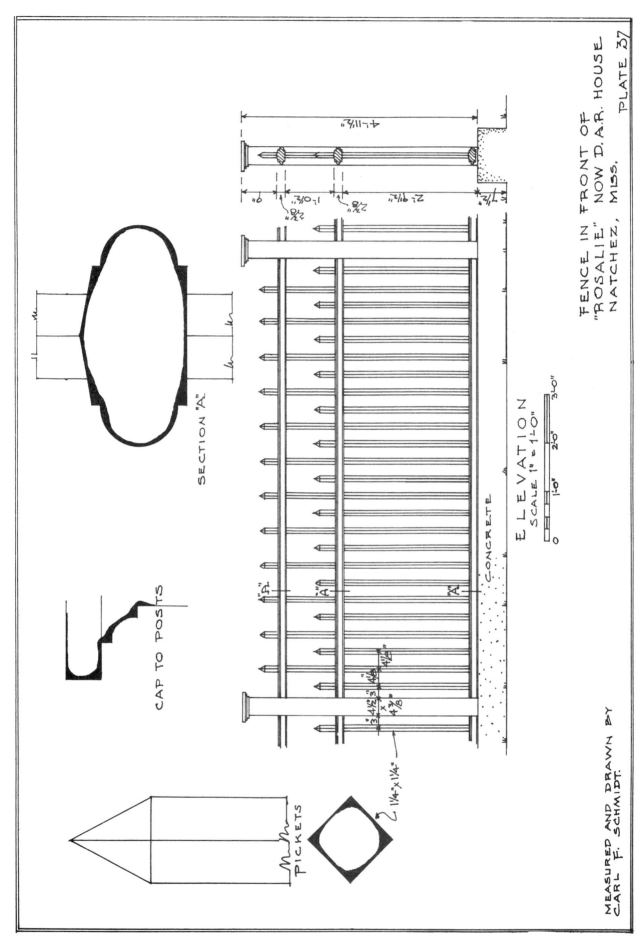

SECTION "A"

CAP TO POSTS

PICKETS

⌐ 1¼"×1¼"

ELEVATION
SCALE 1" = 1'-0"

0   1'-0"   2'-0"   3'-0"

CONCRETE

FENCE IN FRONT OF
"ROSALIE" NOW D.A.R. HOUSE
NATCHEZ, MISS.
PLATE 37

MEASURED AND DRAWN BY
CARL F. SCHMIDT.

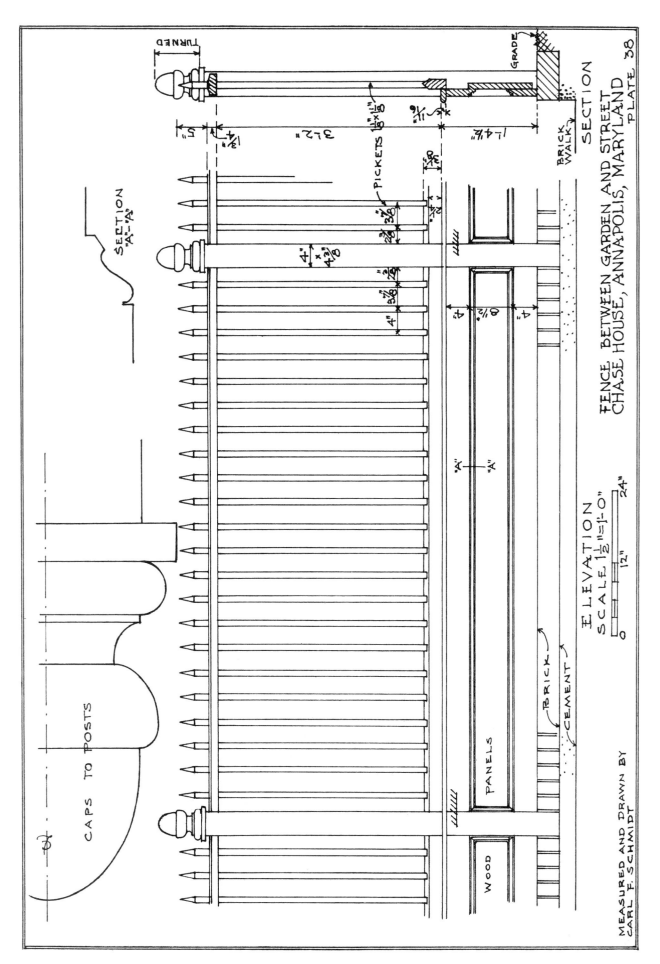

SECTION "A-A"

TURNED

PICKERS $\frac{5}{8}$×1$\frac{1}{8}$"

3'-2"

GRADE

$\frac{1}{2}$"

1$\frac{3}{4}$"

$\frac{5}{8}$"×

SECTION

4" × 4$\frac{3}{8}$"

2$\frac{3}{8}$" 3$\frac{3}{8}$"

2$\frac{1}{2}$"

2$\frac{1}{2}$"

4" 3$\frac{3}{8}$"

4"

1'-4$\frac{3}{8}$"

BRICK WALK

FENCE BETWEEN GARDEN AND STREET
CHASE HOUSE, ANNAPOLIS, MARYLAND
PLATE 38

"A"

"A"

4"

$\frac{5}{8}$"

4"

CAPS TO POSTS

WOOD PANELS

BRICK

CEMENT

ELEVATION
SCALE 1$\frac{1}{2}$"=1'-0"

0   12"   24"

MEASURED AND DRAWN BY
CARL F. SCHMIDT

81

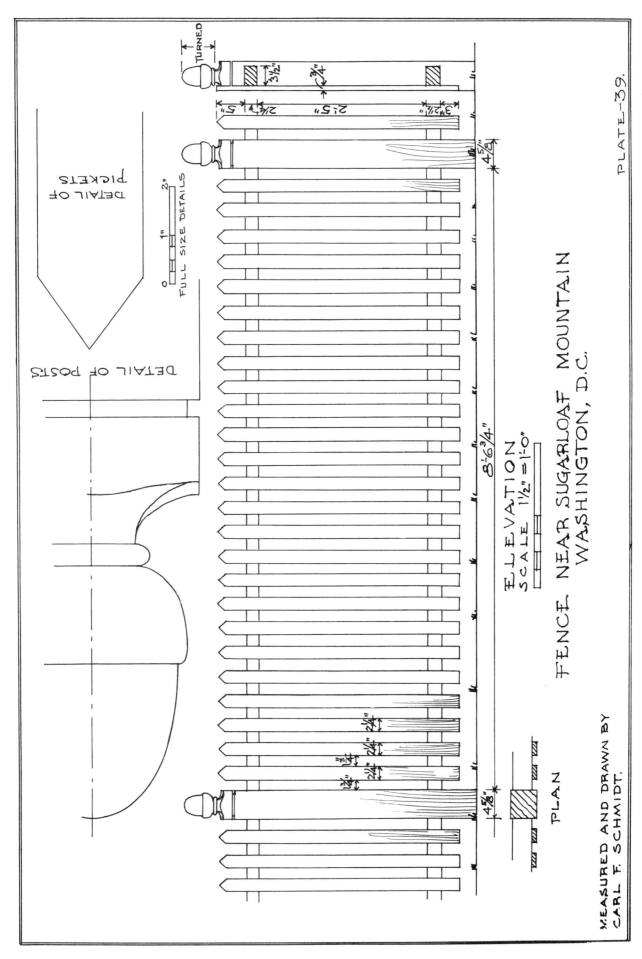

DETAIL OF PICKETS

DETAIL OF POSTS

TURNED

3½"

¾"

5" 2¼"

2'5"

3½2½"

4⅝"

8'6¾"

2¼" 2¼"

2¼" 2¼"

1¾" 1¾"

4⅝"

0 1" 2"

FULL SIZE DETAILS

ELEVATION
SCALE 1½"=1'-0"

PLAN

FENCE NEAR SUGARLOAF MOUNTAIN
WASHINGTON, D.C.

MEASURED AND DRAWN BY
CARL F. SCHMIDT.

PLATE-39.

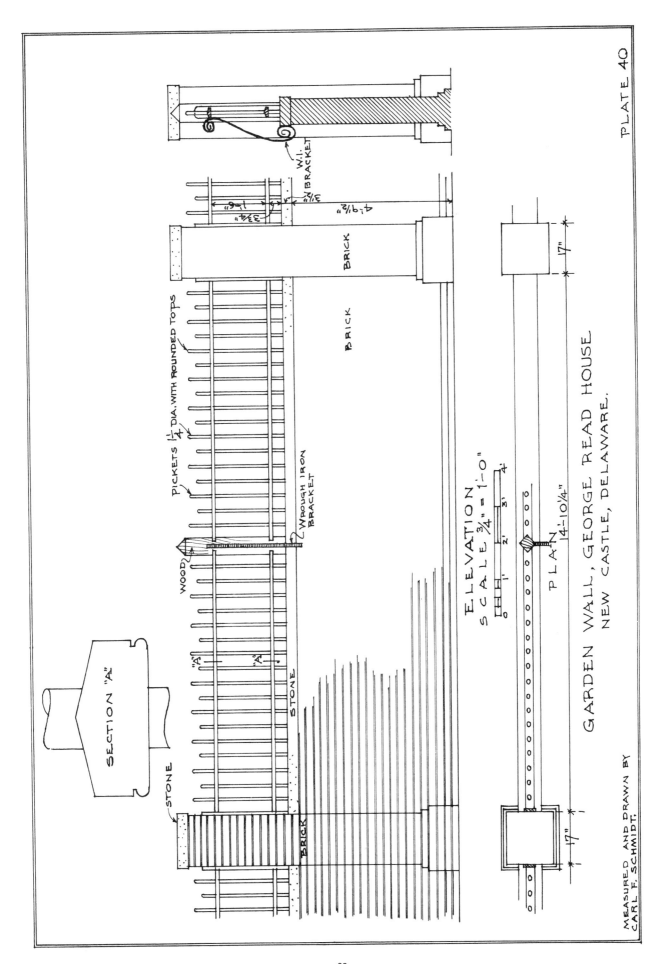

SECTION "A"

STONE

STONE

STONE

BRICK

PICKETS 1¼" DIA. WITH ROUNDED TOPS

WOOD?

WROUGH IRON BRACKET

"A"

"A"

W.I. BRACKET

BRICK

BRICK

1'-6"

3¾"

3½"

4'-9½"

17"

17"

ELEVATION
SCALE ¾" = 1'-0"

0 1' 2' 3' 4'

PLAN
14'-10¼"

GARDEN WALL, GEORGE READ HOUSE
NEW CASTLE, DELAWARE.

MEASURED AND DRAWN BY
CARL F. SCHMIDT.

PLATE 40

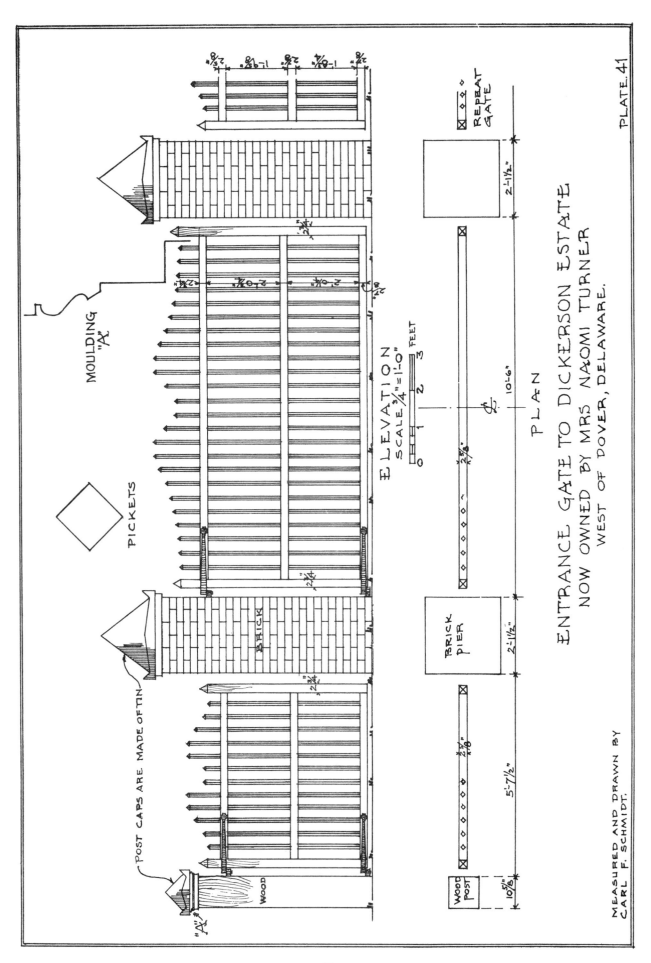

MOULDING "A"

PICKETS

POST CAPS ARE MADE OF TIN

"A"

BRICK

WOOD

ELEVATION
SCALE ¾"=1'-0"

0   1   2   3 FEET

PLAN

BRICK PIER

WOOD POST

REPEAT GATE

ENTRANCE GATE TO DICKERSON ESTATE
NOW OWNED BY MRS NAOMI TURNER
WEST OF DOVER, DELAWARE.

MEASURED AND DRAWN BY
CARL F. SCHMIDT.

PLATE. 41

84

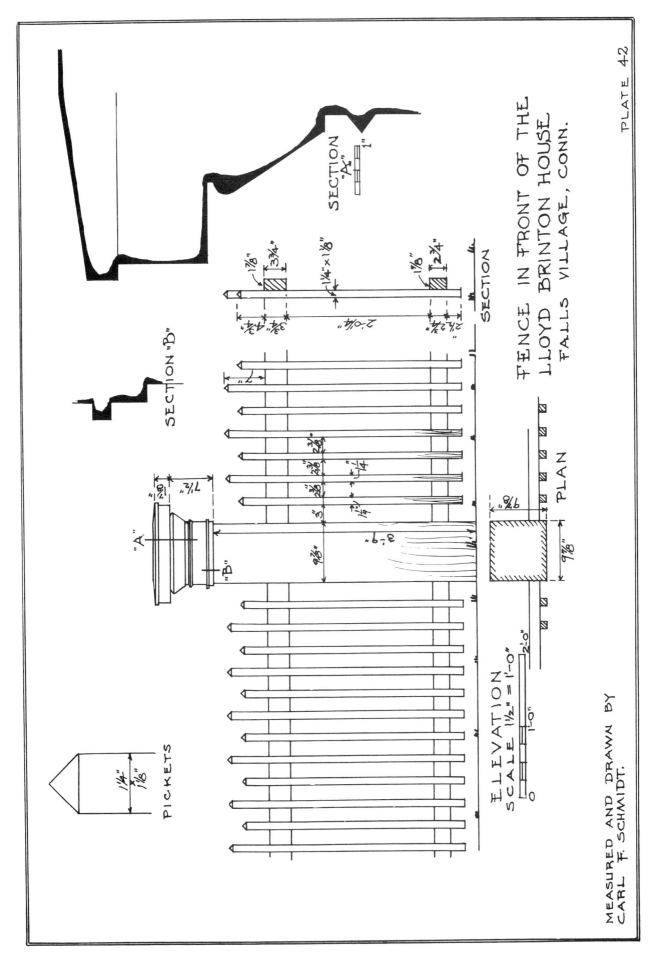

SECTION "A"

SECTION "B"

PICKETS

ELEVATION
SCALE 1½" = 1'-0"

SECTION

PLAN

FENCE IN FRONT OF THE
LLOYD BRINTON HOUSE
FALLS VILLAGE, CONN.

MEASURED AND DRAWN BY
CARL F. SCHMIDT.

PLATE 42

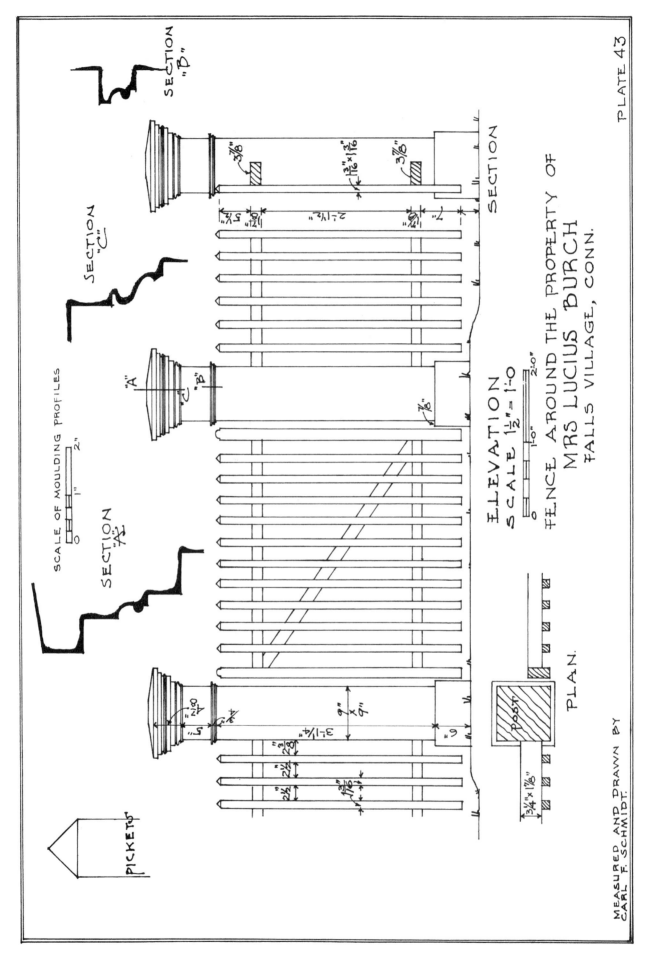

SECTION "B"

SECTION "C"

SECTION "A"

SCALE OF MOULDING PROFILES
0   1"   2"

"A"
"C"   "B"

PICKET.

3/8"

1 3/16" x 1 3/16"

3/8"

5/8"
1 1/4"
2'-1 1/2"
1 1/2"
2"

SECTION

7/8"

ELEVATION
SCALE 1 1/2" = 1'-0

0   1'-0"   2'-0"

FENCE AROUND THE PROPERTY OF
MRS LUCIUS BURCH
FALLS VILLAGE, CONN.

2-0"
4"
5"
2"

9"
X
9"

3'-1 1/4"

6"

2 1/2"
2 1/2"
2 3/8"

1 3/16"

POST

3/4" x 1 7/8"

PLAN.

MEASURED AND DRAWN BY
CARL F. SCHMIDT.

PLATE 43

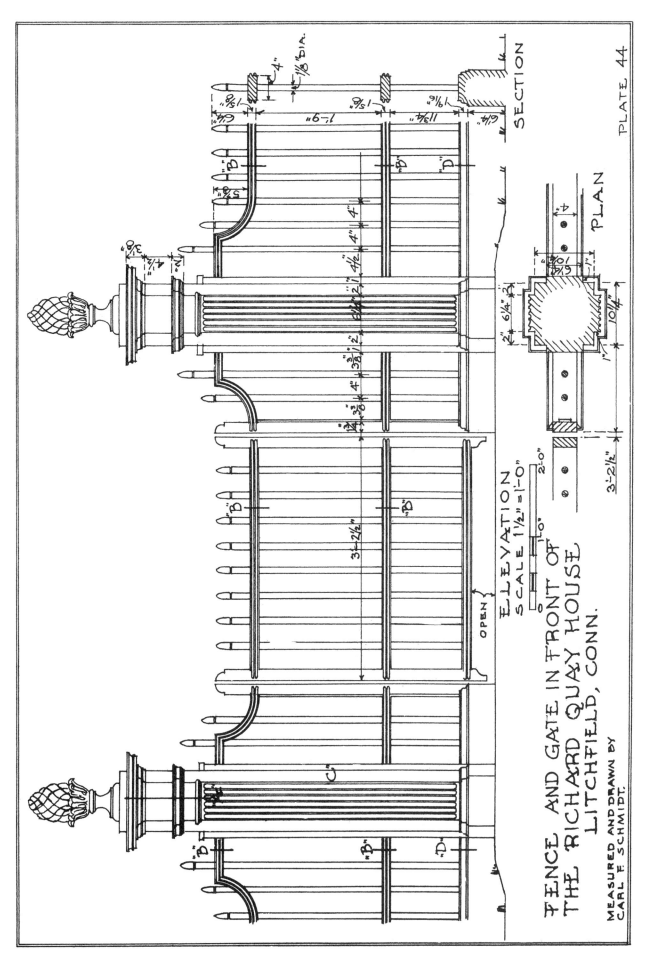

FENCE AND GATE IN FRONT OF
THE RICHARD QUAY HOUSE
LITCHFIELD, CONN.

MEASURED AND DRAWN BY
CARL F. SCHMIDT.

ELEVATION
SCALE 1½" = 1'-0"

SECTION

PLAN

PLATE 44

87

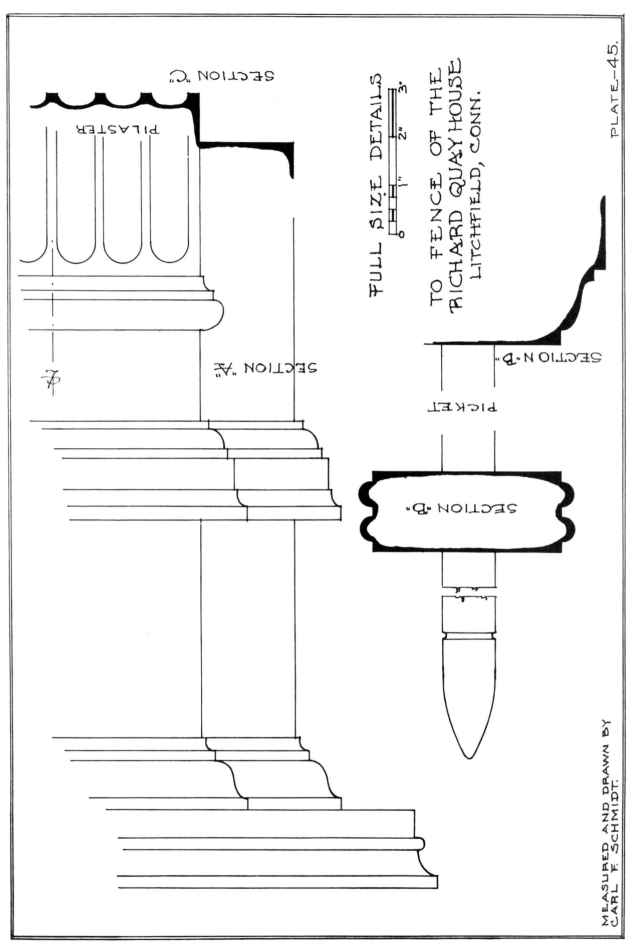

SECTION "C"

PILASTER

SECTION "A"

FULL SIZE DETAILS

TO FENCE OF THE
RICHARD QUAY HOUSE
LITCHFIELD, CONN.

SECTION "B"

PICKET

SECTION "D"

PLATE—45.

MEASURED AND DRAWN BY
CARL F. SCHMIDT.

88

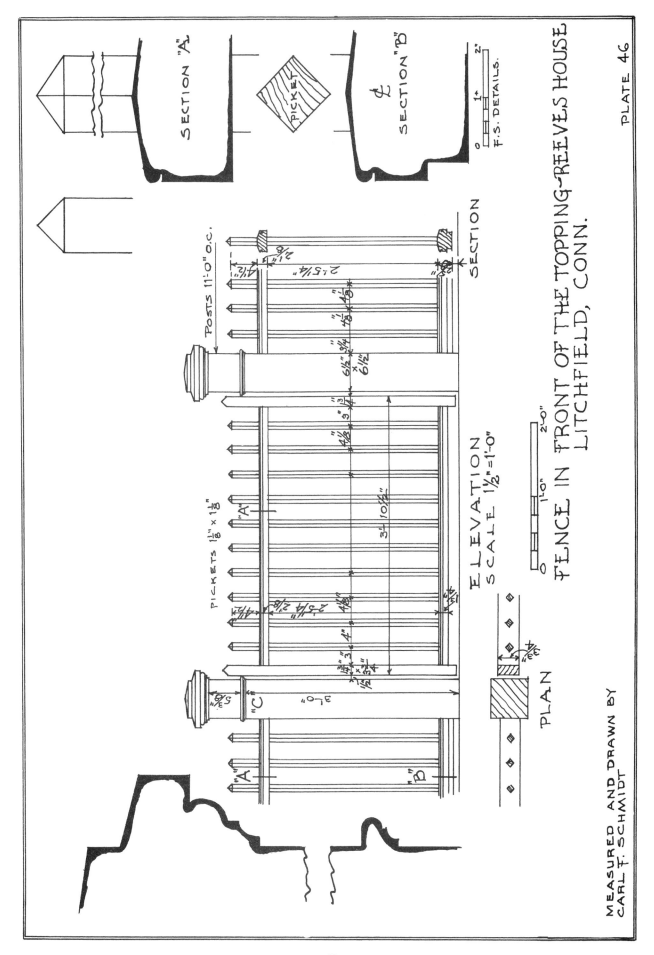

SECTION "A"

PICKET

SECTION "B"

F.S. DETAILS.

0 1" 2"

SECTION

POSTS 11'-0" O.C.

PICKETS 1⅛" × 1⅛"

"A"

"A"

"C"

3'-0"

"B"

PLAN

ELEVATION
SCALE 1½"=1'-0"

0 1'-0" 2'-0"

FENCE IN FRONT OF THE TOPPING-REEVES HOUSE
LITCHFIELD, CONN.

PLATE 46

MEASURED AND DRAWN BY
CARL F. SCHMIDT

89

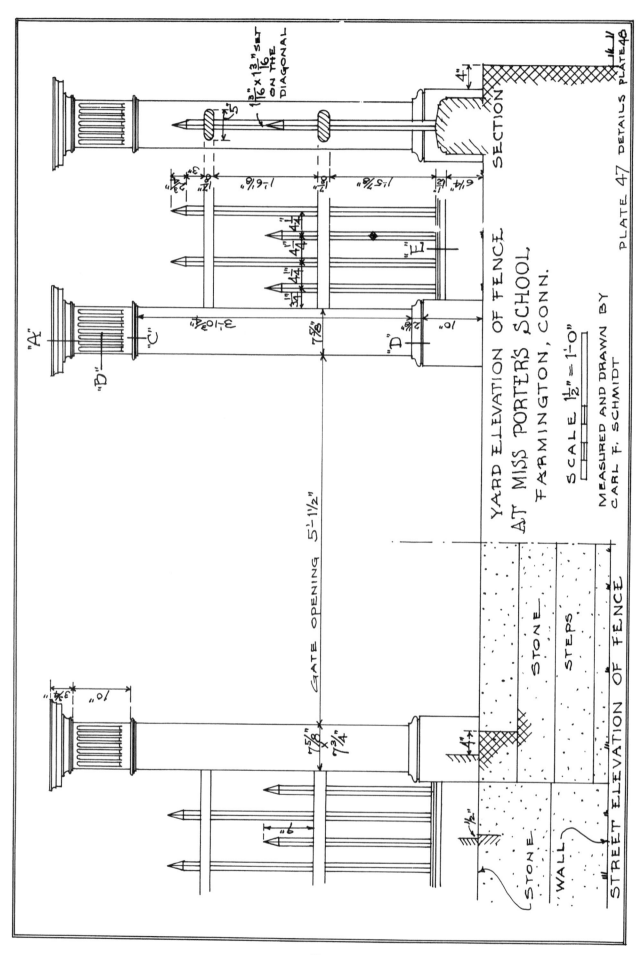

SECTION

$1\frac{13}{16}" \times 1\frac{13}{16}"$ SET ON THE DIAGONAL

"A"

"B"

"C"

"D"

"E"

GATE OPENING 5'-1½"

YARD ELEVATION OF FENCE
AT MISS PORTER'S SCHOOL
FARMINGTON, CONN.

SCALE 1½" = 1'-0"

MEASURED AND DRAWN BY
CARL F. SCHMIDT

PLATE 47 DETAILS PLATE 48

STONE
STEPS

STONE
WALL

STREET ELEVATION OF FENCE

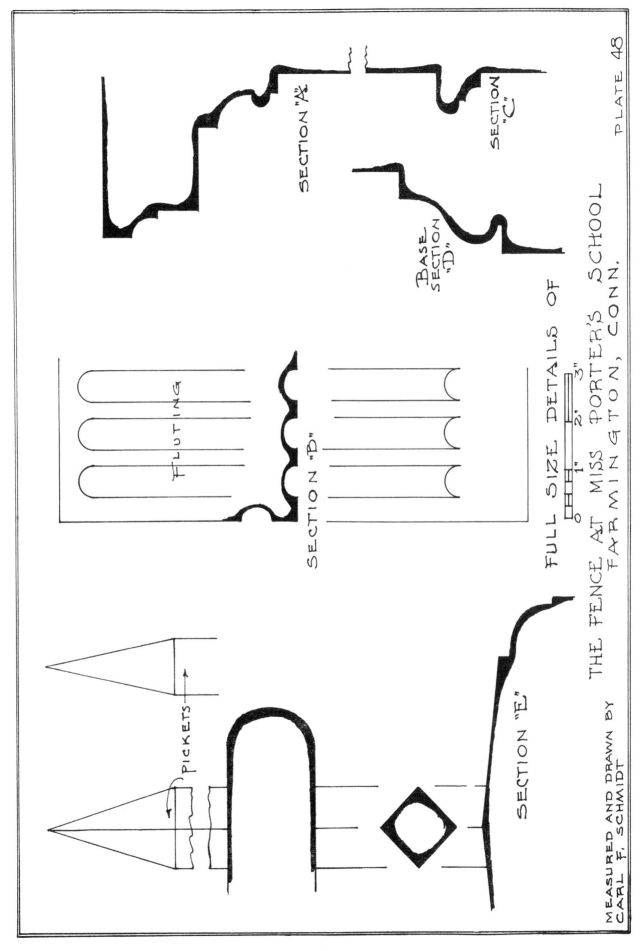

SECTION "A"

SECTION "C"

BASE
SECTION
"D"

FLUTING

SECTION "B"

PICKETS

SECTION "E"

FULL SIZE DETAILS OF

0 1" 2" 3"

THE FENCE AT MISS PORTER'S SCHOOL
FARMINGTON, CONN.

MEASURED AND DRAWN BY
CARL F. SCHMIDT

PLATE 48

91

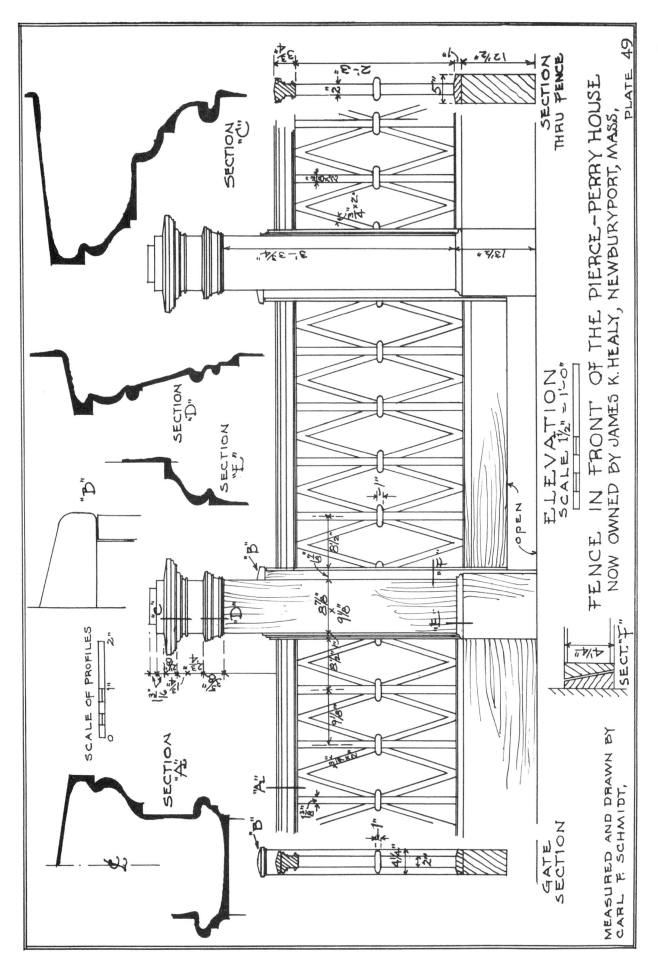

SECTION "C"

SECTION "D"

SECTION "E"

"B"

SCALE OF PROFILES

0   1"   2"

SECTION "A"

SECTION THRU FENCE

PLATE 49

ELEVATION
SCALE 1½" = 1'-0"

FENCE IN FRONT OF THE PIERCE-PERRY HOUSE
NOW OWNED BY JAMES K. HEALY, NEWBURYPORT, MASS.

GATE
SECTION

MEASURED AND DRAWN BY
CARL F. SCHMIDT,

92

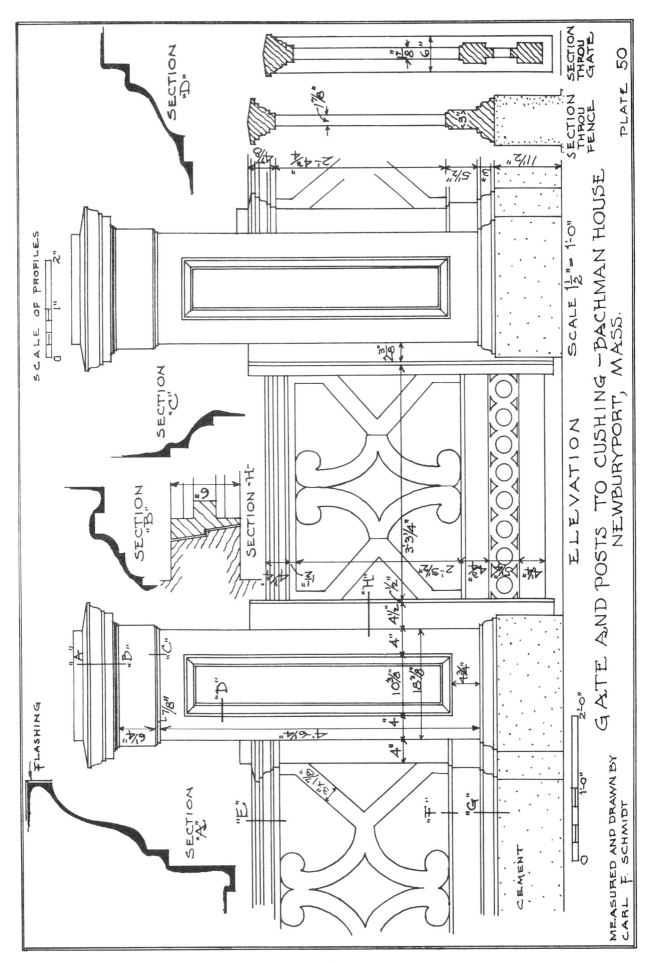

SECTION "D"

SECTION THROU GATE

SECTION THROU FENCE

PLATE 50

SCALE OF PROFILES

SECTION "C"

SECTION "B"

SECTION "H"

FLASHING

SECTION "A"

ELEVATION   SCALE 1½" = 1'-0"

GATE AND POSTS TO CUSHING — BACHMAN HOUSE
NEWBURYPORT, MASS.

MEASURED AND DRAWN BY
CARL F. SCHMIDT

CEMENT

93

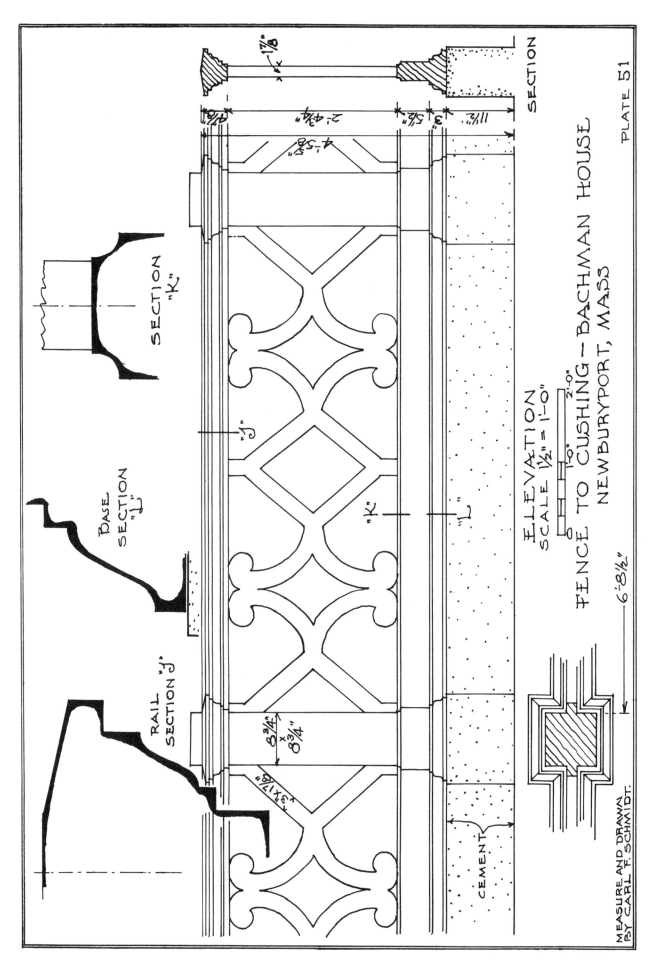

SECTION "K"

SECTION

RAIL SECTION "J"

BASE SECTION "L"

8¾" x 8¾"

4⅝" x 17½"

4'-5½"

2'-4¾"

1⅞"

CEMENT

ELEVATION
SCALE 1½" = 1'-0"

FENCE TO CUSHING — BACHMAN HOUSE
NEWBURYPORT, MASS

PLATE 51

MEASURE AND DRAWN
BY CARL F. SCHMIDT.

6'-8½"

2'-0"

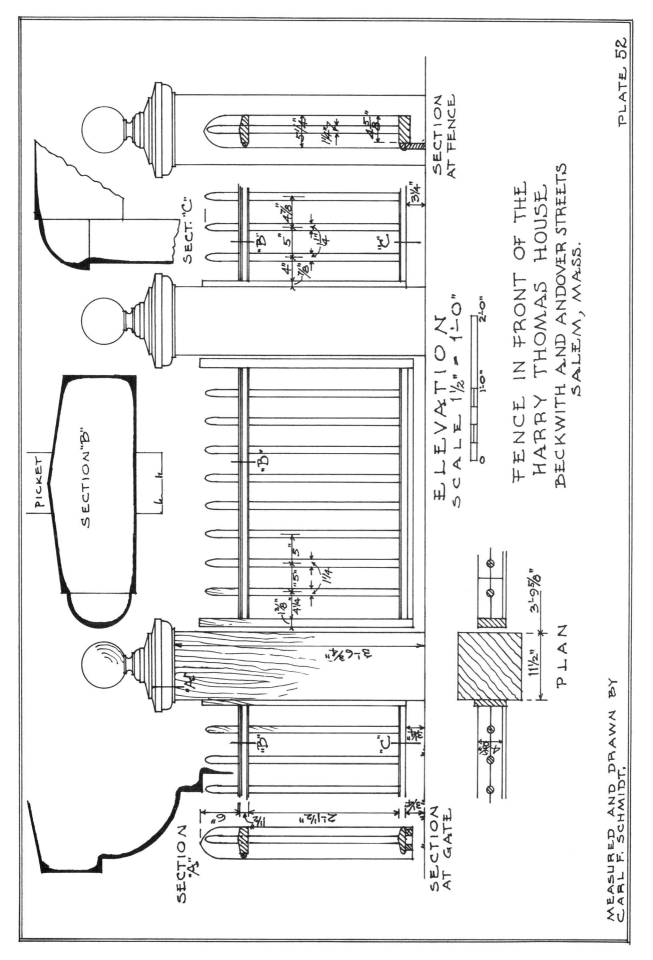

PICKET

SECTION "B"

SECTION "C"

SECTION "A"

SECT. "C"

"B"

"C"

SECTION AT FENCE

SECTION AT GATE

PLAN

ELEVATION
SCALE 1½" = 1'-0"

0   1'-0"   2'-0"

FENCE IN FRONT OF THE
HARRY THOMAS HOUSE,
BECKWITH AND ANDOVER STREETS
SALEM, MASS.

MEASURED AND DRAWN BY
CARL F. SCHMIDT.

PLATE 52

95

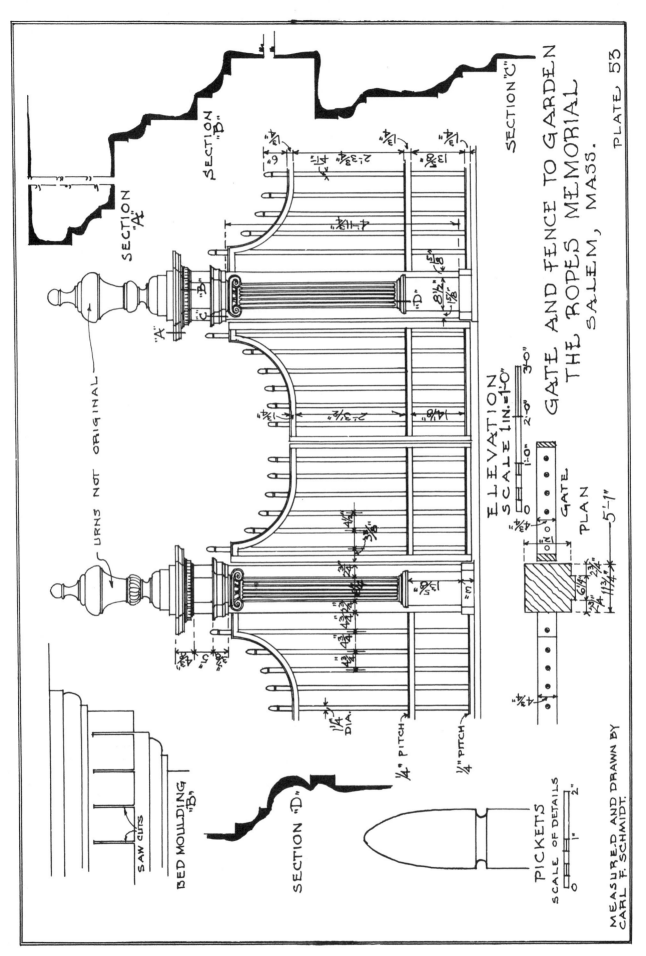

SECTION "C"

SECTION "B"

SECTION "A"

URNS NOT ORIGINAL

BED MOULDING "B"

SAW CUTS

SECTION "D"

¼" PITCH

¼" PITCH

ELEVATION
SCALE 1 IN.=1'-0"

0   1'-0"   2'-0"   3'-0"

GATE
PLAN

5'-1"

PICKETS
SCALE OF DETAILS

0   1"   2"

GATE AND FENCE TO GARDEN
THE ROPES MEMORIAL
SALEM, MASS.

PLATE 53

MEASURED AND DRAWN BY
CARL F. SCHMIDT.

96

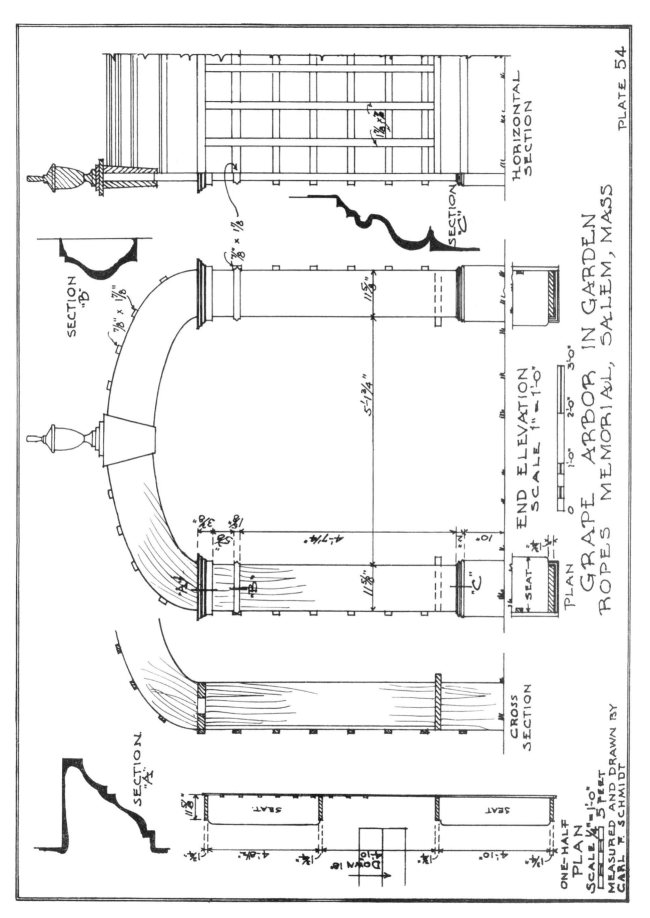

HORIZONTAL SECTION

PLATE 54

SECTION "C"

1½" x 3"

⅞" x 1⅛"

SECTION "B"

⅞" x 1⅛"

END ELEVATION
SCALE 1" = 1'-0"

GRAPE ARBOR IN GARDEN
ROPES MEMORIAL, SALEM, MASS

5'-1¾"

11⅝"

0 1'-0" 2'-0" 3'-0"

3⅜"

1⅝"

4'-7⅛"

11⅝"

2"

10"

PLAN

SEAT

"C"

CROSS SECTION

SECTION "A"

ONE-HALF
PLAN
SCALE ¼"=1'-0" 5 FEET

MEASURED AND DRAWN BY
CARL F. SCHMIDT

SEAT

SEAT

DOWN 16

11⅝"

¾"

4'-10"

1⅛"

4'-6½"

1¾"

¾"

97

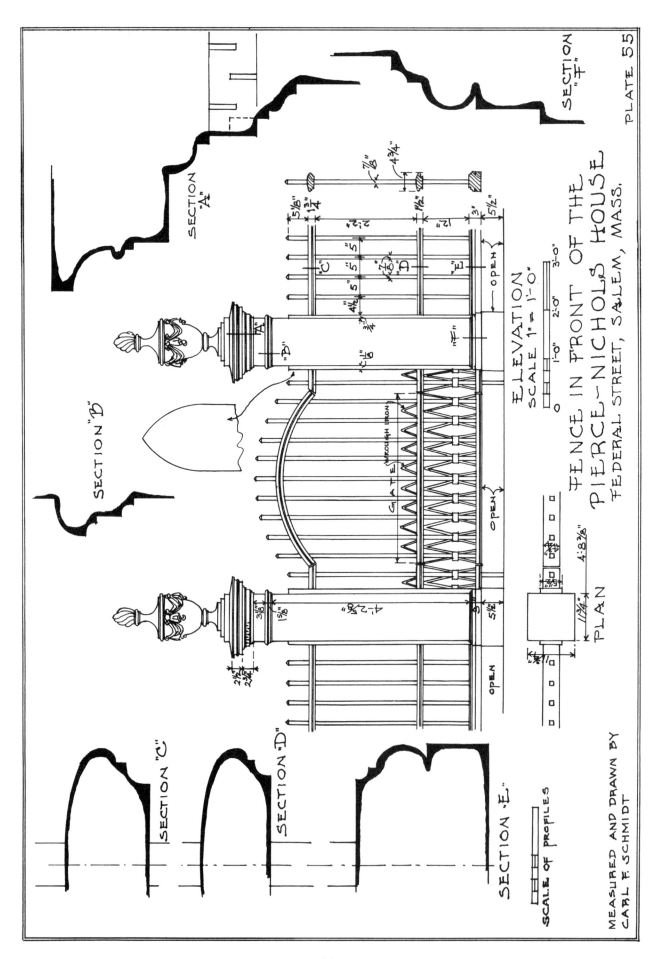

SECTION "A"

SECTION "F"

PLATE 55

SECTION "B"

SECTION "C"

SECTION "D"

SECTION "E"

5/8"
1 3/4"

5"   5"   5"

4 1/2"

3/4"

5 1/2"

7/8"

4 3/4"

1 1/2"

3"

5 1/2"

OPEN

OPEN

GATE (WROUGHT IRON)

"C"

"D"

"E"

2 1/8"

"D"

2 1/2"
2 3/4"

3 1/8"

1 5/8"

4'-2 5/8"

5"

5 1/2"

OPEN

4'-8 7/8"

1 3/4"

PLAN

ELEVATION
SCALE 1"=1'-0"

0   1'-0"   2'-0"   3'-0"

FENCE IN FRONT OF THE
PIERCE-NICHOLS HOUSE,
FEDERAL STREET, SALEM, MASS.

SCALE OF PROFILES

MEASURED AND DRAWN BY
CARL F. SCHMIDT

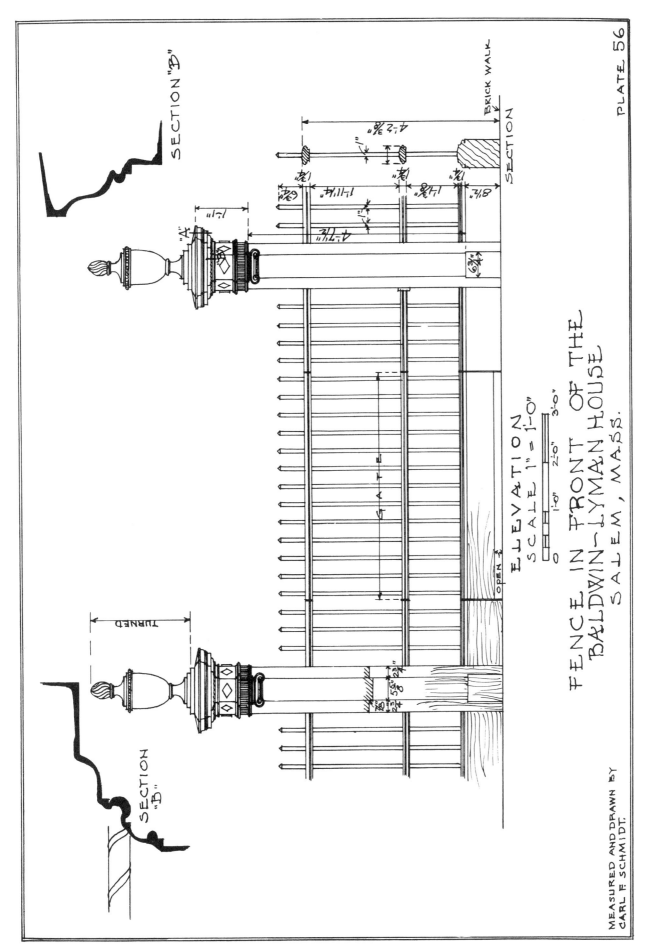

SECTION "B"

SECTION "B"

TURNED

"A"

GATE

OPEN

BRICK WALK

SECTION

ELEVATION
SCALE 1" = 1'-0"

0 1'-0" 2'-0" 3'-0"

FENCE IN FRONT OF THE
BALDWIN-LYMAN HOUSE
SALEM, MASS.

MEASURED AND DRAWN BY
CARL F. SCHMIDT.

PLATE 56

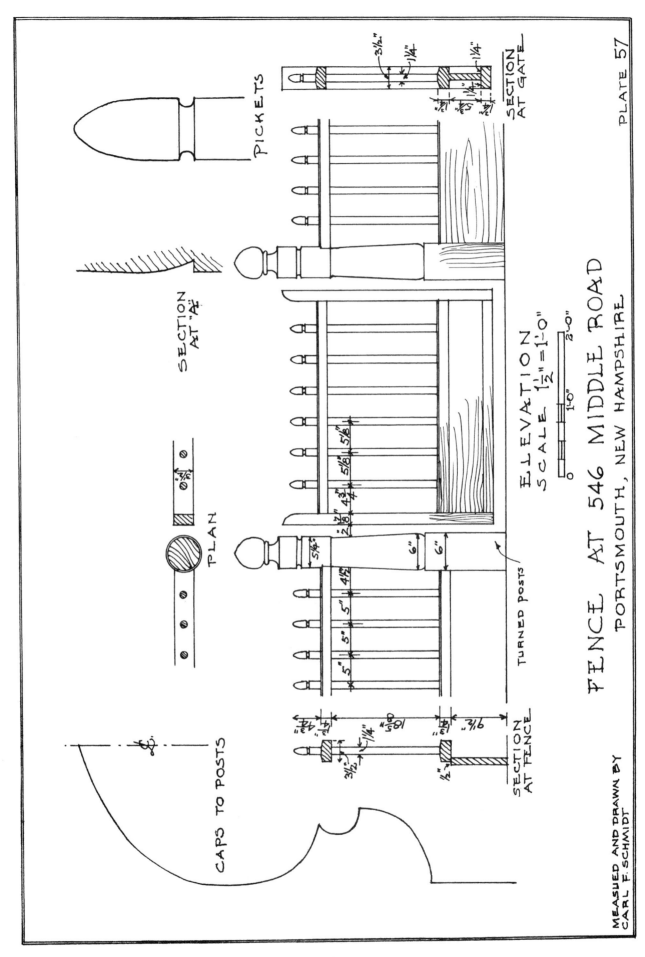

PICKETS

SECTION AT GATE

SECTION AT "A"

PLAN

SECTION AT FENCE

TURNED POSTS

CAPS TO POSTS

ELEVATION
SCALE 1½"=1'-0"

0   1'-0"   2'-0"

FENCE AT 546 MIDDLE ROAD
PORTSMOUTH, NEW HAMPSHIRE

MEASURED AND DRAWN BY
CARL F. SCHMIDT

PLATE 57

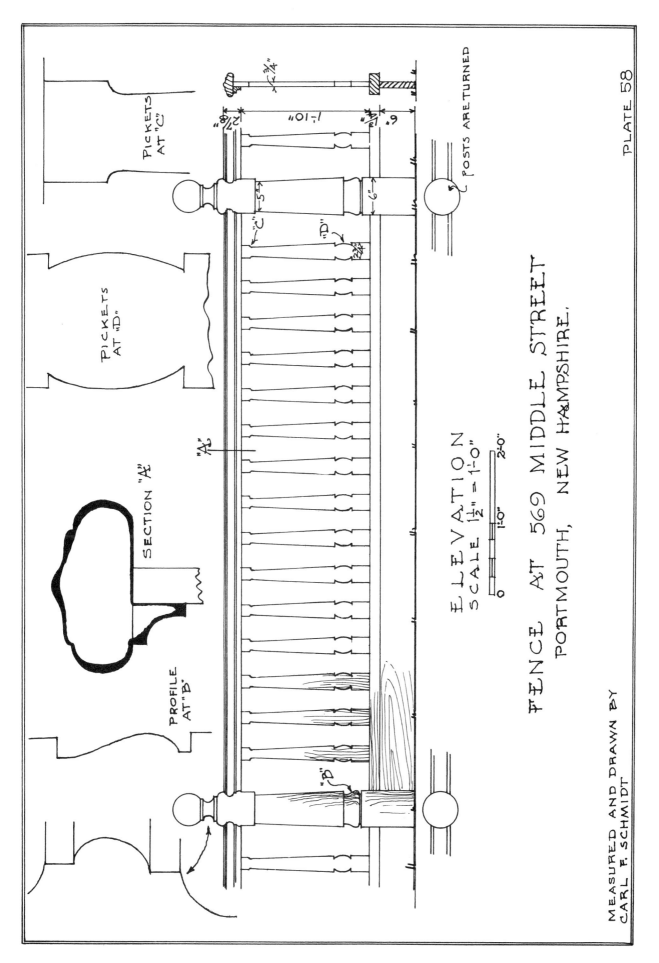

PICKETS AT "C"

PICKETS AT "D"

SECTION "A"

PROFILE AT "B"

POSTS ARE TURNED

ELEVATION
SCALE 1½" = 1'-0"

0   1'-0"   2'-0"

FENCE AT 569 MIDDLE STREET
PORTMOUTH, NEW HAMPSHIRE.

MEASURED AND DRAWN BY
CARL F. SCHMIDT

PLATE 58

101

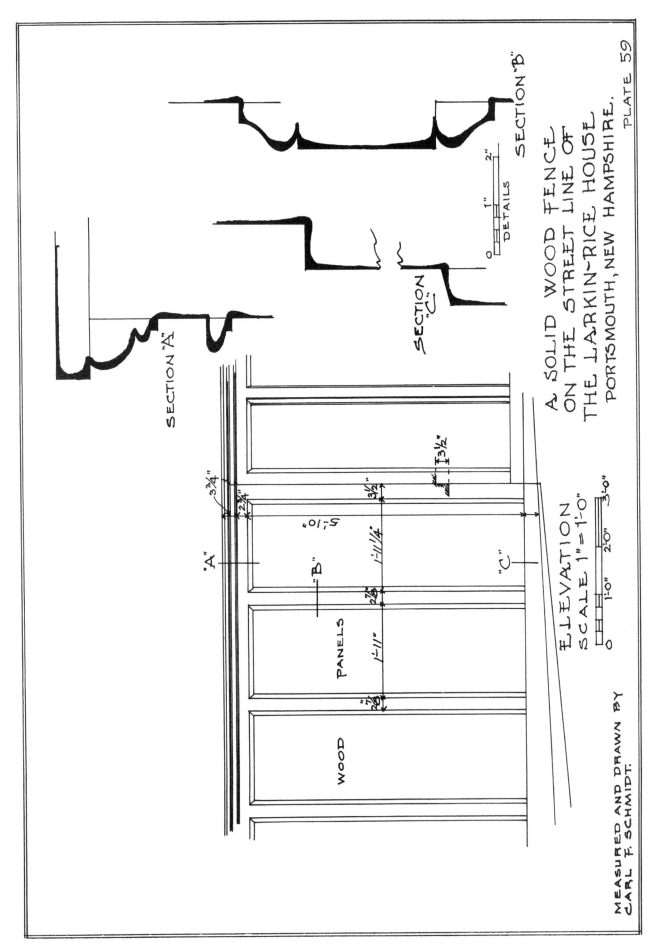

SECTION "A"

SECTION "B"

SECTION "C"

DETAILS

0 1" 2"

A SOLID WOOD FENCE
ON THE STREET LINE OF
THE LARKIN-RICE HOUSE.
PORTSMOUTH, NEW HAMPSHIRE.

PLATE 59

3¾"
2¼"
3½"
3½"
5'-10"
1'-11¼"
2⅝"
1'-11"
2⅝"

"A"
"B"
"C"
WOOD PANELS

ELEVATION
SCALE 1"=1'-0"

0 1'-0" 2'-0" 3'-0"

MEASURED AND DRAWN BY
CARL F. SCHMIDT.

102

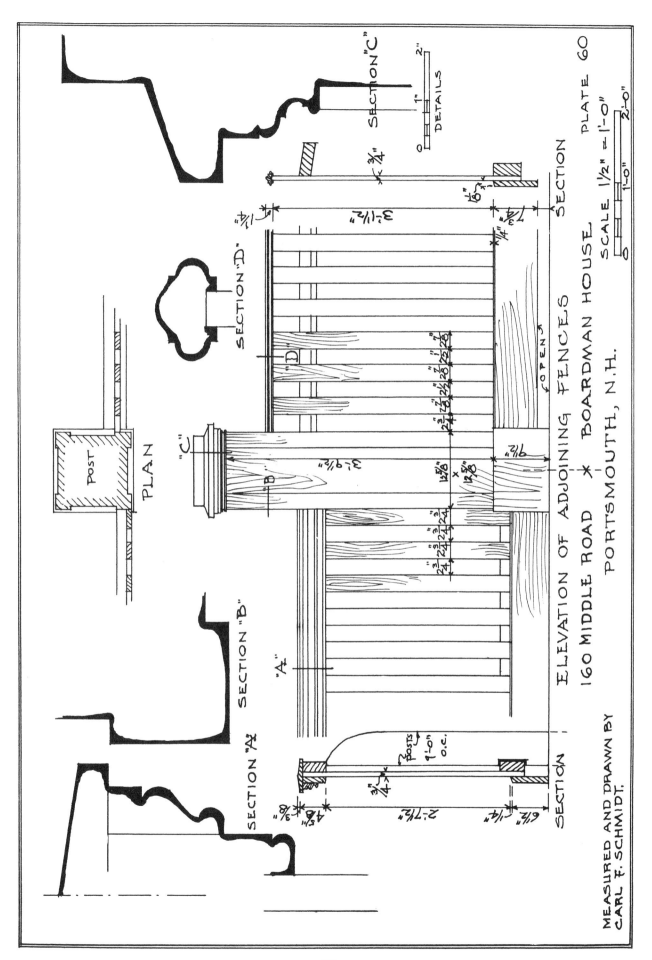

SECTION "C"

2"

DETAILS

1"

0

SECTION "D"

3'-11½"

¾"

⅛"

½"

¾"

SECTION

PLAN

POST

"C"

"B"

3'-9½"

"D"

2 3/4" 2" 2" 1" 1"
24 24½ 25 25 26

12 5/8"
×
12 5/8"

9½"

3/4" 3" 3" 3"
24 24½ 24½
23

"A"

SECTION "B"

SECTION "A"

POSTS 1'-0" o.c.

3/4"

⅜"

4 5/8"

6½" 1½"

2'-7½"

SECTION

ELEVATION OF ADJOINING FENCES ✳ BOARDMAN HOUSE

160 MIDDLE ROAD   PORTSMOUTH, N.H.

PLATE 60

SCALE 1½" = 1'-0"

1'-0"

0

2'-0"

MEASURED AND DRAWN BY
CARL F. SCHMIDT.

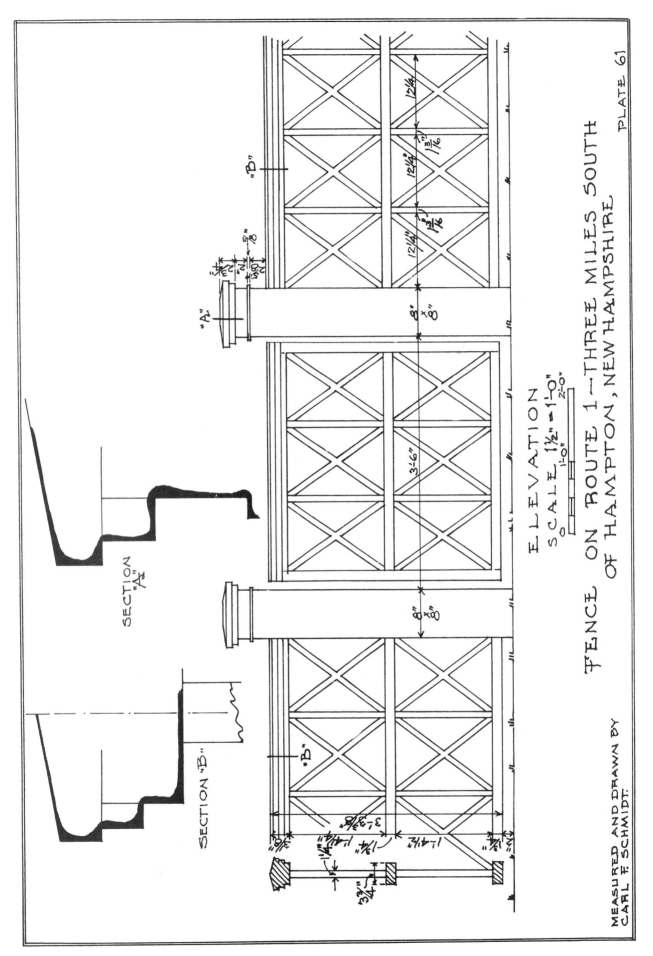

ELEVATION

SCALE 1½" = 1'-0"

FENCE ON ROUTE 1—THREE MILES SOUTH OF HAMPTON, NEW HAMPSHIRE

PLATE 61

SECTION "A"

SECTION "B"

MEASURED AND DRAWN BY
CARL F. SCHMIDT

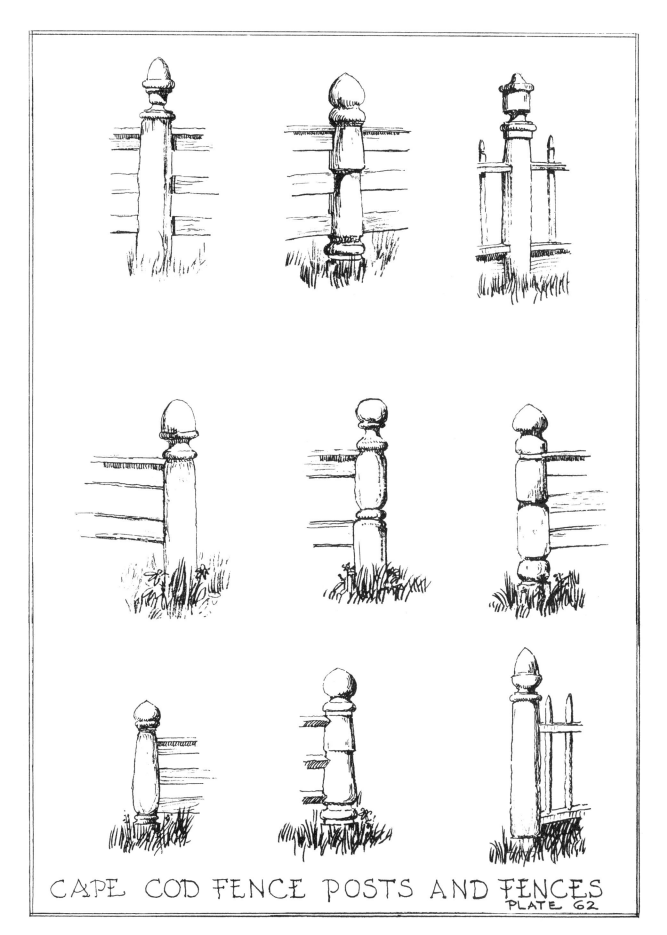

CAPE COD FENCE POSTS AND FENCES

PLATE 62

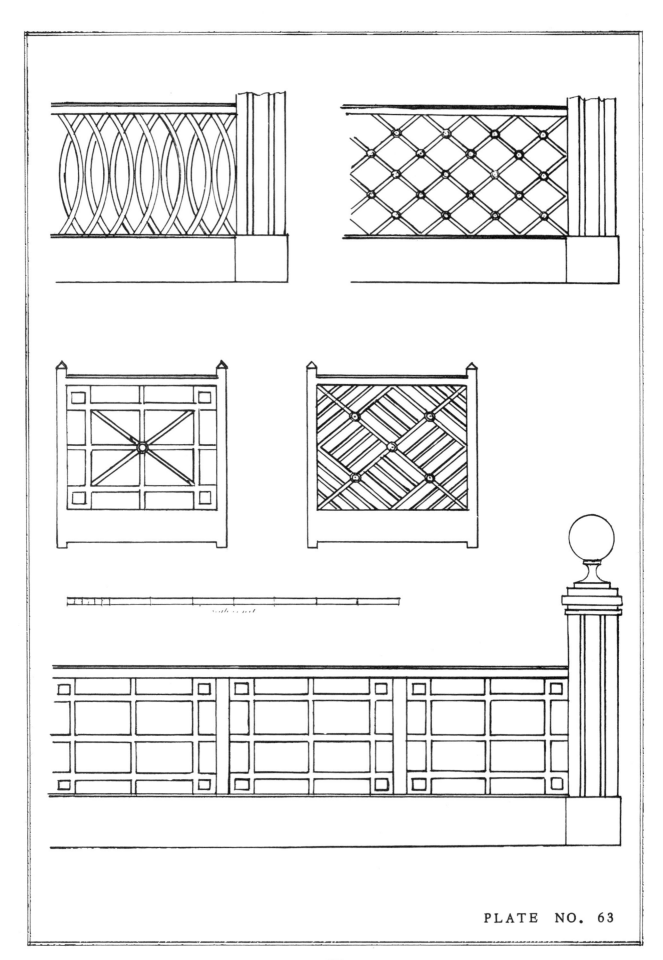

PLATE NO. 63